PICK UP
THE
PHONE
AND
SELL

ALEX GOLDFAYN

Wall Street Journal Bestselling Author of 5-Minute Selling

PICK UP
THE
PHONE
AND
SELL

HOW PROACTIVE CALLS
TO CUSTOMERS AND PROSPECTS
CAN DOUBLE YOUR SALES

WILEY

Published by John Wiley & Sons, Inc., Hoboken, New Jersey.

Published simultaneously in Canada.

Library of Congress Cataloging-in-Publication Data is Available:

ISBN 9781119814603 (Hardcover)
ISBN 9781119814641 (ePDF)
ISBN 9781119814658 (ePub)

Cover design: PAUL MCCARTHY

SKY10028663_081121

To my mom, Jane Goldfayn, who makes proactive calls to me every single day.

She was the first writer in the family.

CONTENTS

Part One: Introduction

Part Two: Your Mindset and Your Phone

Part Three: Call Tactics, Mechanics, and Strategies

Part Five: Cold Calls: Calling People You Don't Know ...Yet

PICK UP THE PHONE AND SELL

PART ONE

INTRODUCTION

CHAPTER

1

The Lost Art of Proactive Calling in the Sales Profession

This is the most obvious book I've ever written.

You're reading my fifth book on sales growth, but none has been as clearly necessary and important to write as this one. Especially now, in a post-pandemic world, where we cannot see our customers nearly as much as we previously could.

In the selling profession, only the phone is so universally understood to be *the* key to success and, at the same time, so widely avoided. A surprisingly large number of salespeople even dread it.

In the 1980s and so many of the decades that came before, if you wanted to sit in your office and communicate with a lot of people quickly, the only option you had was the wired landline telephone.

So a lot of salespeople had no choice but to be really good at using the phone.

In the late 1990s, we got email. It was faster. And easier.

And, over time, many of us moved to email as our preferred method of communicating with customers and prospects.

Then we got cell phones.

And text messages.

And then social media rolled in:

We could have Facebook pages.

And LinkedIn connections.

And we could tweet at people.

All of these things were also faster, easier, and far less threatening than the phone.

So we went to them.

Because on these platforms, rejection is usually simply silence, whereas on the phone, it's intimate and personal and spoken directly into our ears.

Of course, we still have meetings, and we're good at them because we never really stopped having them.

But how many meetings can you have in a day? About as many as an hour's worth of phone conversations.

And so, over the last few "Internet decades," the entire sales profession has moved away from what so many used to excel at: proactive phone calls to customers and prospects.

What's a *proactive* call?

Communicating by phone with customers and prospects when nothing is wrong.

I run a large solo consulting practice, working with business-to-business organizations to grow their sales. My clients average 10–20% in additional new sales growth annually directly from our work together. Even large companies, in mature industries. Even companies that have been stagnant and have not added significantly to their sales in years. Even these companies add 10–20% in new sales.

Individually, many salespeople double and sometimes even triple their sales when applying the techniques I teach them – techniques I lay out in this book.

How would doubling your sales numbers improve your life?

Or maybe "only" increasing them by 50% . . . what would that do for you and your family?

How do my client salespeople achieve this kind of growth?

Centrally, with the phone.

By letting customers and prospects hear from them proactively.

By being present.

By being interested.

By demonstrating that they care.

How?

Almost entirely with the phone.

Before the pandemic, I did 75 to 100 speeches and workshops each year focused on my techniques for sales growth.

When the pandemic besieged us, I continued doing live sessions virtually, but because salespeople couldn't see their customers any more, I doubled down on how to use the phone to grow sales.

Many of these sessions were in multiple parts – often a series of three sessions, with the same audience each time.

By the third webinar, after spending at least two hours exploring the ins and outs of telephone selling, I would ask the attendees what they'd like me to focus on. I like to go where my audiences want me to go.

I would even give options:

Do you want to talk about selling more to existing customers?
Or asking for referrals?
Or following up on quotes or proposals?
What about asking for the business?
Or do you want me to go over phone selling some more? (Keep in mind, this was the dominant topic of the previous two sessions these same people had attended.)

Via the chat function, people made their requests. The vast majority of topics salespeople wanted to cover centered on selling over the phone:

When should we call?
Who should we call?
What if we don't have the customer's cell phone number?
Do I leave a voice message?
How many times should I try before giving up?

And then, inevitably, these kinds of comments would be raised:

I don't like selling on the phone, but I know I need to.
I hate getting cold calls.
I don't have time to call people.
Nobody returns my calls anyway.

These questions and comments illustrate the obvious: there is a hunger for instruction on how to sell with the phone. And there is discomfort about doing it.

We've gotten away from using the phone as a selling tool, but innately, we know how useful and effective it can be.

To complicate matters, there is a dearth of resources on this topic.

Search for books about social media selling, and you'll find hundreds of them – and thousands of blogs and podcasts, and tens of thousands of "experts" on the subject. (Ironic, since business-to-business selling success over social media is extremely challenging.)

But try to find a recent book on phone selling, and you will have very few choices.

In fact, you can count on one hand the phone-selling books that have been written in the last decade.

And not one of them looks at selling with the phone in combination with the digital tools at our disposal: virtual meeting tools like Zoom, text messaging, email, and, yes, social media like LinkedIn.

Want to look for a blog or podcast about phone selling? When I Google "phone selling," I get "selling old cell phones for cash."

So, I wrote *Pick Up the Phone and Sell.*

My goal is to arm you with a quick and simple guide for attaining significant sales growth by proactively calling your customers and prospects.

Get good at using the phone, and you will be in rare air in the sales profession.

Because the great majority of salespeople are not very good at using the phone.

I'd say 90% of salespeople are reactive in our work.

We're very good at *answering* the phone and solving problems.

But not many of us regularly pick up the phone to call customers and prospects proactively when nothing is wrong.

This is where relationships are built.

This is where trust is formed.

This is where you get to help your customers and expand your business with them.

This is where the money is made.

The rare salesperson who regularly and systematically makes proactive calls gets to *stack* these successes one on top of the other, with customer after customer.

Among my clients, the salespeople who most often proactively call customers and prospects are the most successful salespeople in their organizations.

Ninety percent of salespeople are reactive and don't call.

Want to launch yourself instantly into the top 10% of all salespeople?

Follow the approaches you're about to read, and leverage the power of proactive calls.

There's a book for that now!

DOWNLOAD YOUR *PICK UP THE PHONE AND SELL* TOOLS

The tools, forms, planners, and trackers that appear throughout this book are available as a free download at my website, www.Goldfayn.com.

You can also get various tools there, like my sales growth instructional videos and free weekly email newsletter.

Go to Goldfayn.com and arm yourself with the resources to pick up the phone and grow your sales.

CHAPTER

An Executive Summary: How to Pick Up the Phone and Sell

H ere is a lightning-fast executive summary of the approaches laid out in this book:

In my experience with tens of thousands of salespeople, clients, and workshop attendees applying my sales growth approaches, the single most effective – and avoided – selling action is the phone call.

I believe that we salespeople should **lead with the phone**.

That is, it should be the first action in our selling day and also the first effort in our selling sequence with individual customers. At the start of your week, make a quick plan of who to call.

Call first. The reasons why are in the next chapter.

Create your Target 60 list of customers and prospects to focus on for the coming month. This planner is presented in Chapter 7.

Next, lay out your Simple Proactive Call Planner for the week, identifying current and past customers you will call, and current and past prospects. This planner is also in Chapter 7.

Aim to call three to five customers or prospects per day, first thing in the morning.

Who should you call? **First, call people who you know –** current and former customers, and current and former prospects. Call people who recognize your name or at least your company name. Too many people assume proactive calls only mean cold calls. In fact, you can grow your sales dramatically by *only calling people you know and offering to help them (more)*.

We will revisit this in Chapter 23, but for now, these are the people you should be thinking about calling proactively, with the groups in order from right to left – always focusing on the people who know you or at least recognize you or your company.

If you prefer, **send a quick text in advance to set a time to speak**.

When you call, you will frequently need to **leave a voice message** (scripts are in Chapter 19), which you should absolutely do.

After leaving the message, send a short text to let the customer know you called, and invite them to get back to you by text or phone, whichever is easier for them. This gives them a *choice* of how to communicate with you.

With this voicemail-text message communication combination, you will find that about two-thirds of your customers and prospects will get back to you.

On the off chance that the customer picks up the phone, great; you will have a nice, positive conversation. (Simple scripts are throughout Parts 4 and 5.)

Log your communication in the Proactive Call Tracker featured in this book or your own action-tracking or CRM system.

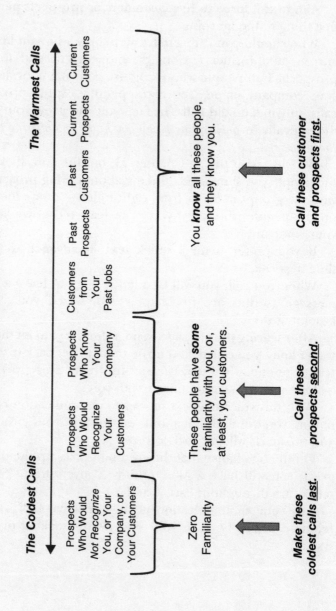

Who to Call:
The Warmest & Coldest Proactive Calls

The Coldest Calls

The Warmest Calls

| Prospects Who Would *Not Recognize* You, or Your Company, or Your Customers | Prospects Who Would *Recognize* Your Customers | Prospects Who Know Your Company | Customers from Your Past Jobs | Past Prospects | Past Customers | Current Prospects | Current Customers |

Zero Familiarity

These people have *some* familiarity with you, or, at least, your customers.

You *know* all these people, and they know you.

Make these coldest calls last.

Call these prospects second.

Call these customer and prospects first.

Log the return communications as well, so you remember who you have reached out to and who got back to you.

Update your pipeline daily, because this approach will create countless opportunities for you, as well as a daily progression of customers and prospects toward a quote, a proposal, or a close; and, of course, you'll be securing a lot of new business.

It all starts with a proactive call to a customer or prospect when nothing is wrong.

Make that the tip of your selling spear.

Make it the first action.

And then start making plans for a sudden and significant influx of new business, because the floodgates are about to open.

CHAPTER

3

Lead with the Phone: Make It the Tip of Your Selling Spear

DEFINITION: WHAT IS A PROACTIVE CALL?

The *proactive phone call*, for our purposes in this book, is defined as calling customers and prospects when nothing is wrong.

Your call can be scheduled with a text message.

While many salespeople only talk on the phone when the customer calls them, this generally focuses the conversation on problems you need to resolve. But this book is about calling the customers proactively, which almost always becomes a conversation about opportunities for you to help the customer.

PROACTIVE CALLS FEED THE SALES MACHINE

Proactive calls feed the machine of your business growth:

- They flood your pipeline with new opportunities and advance existing ones.

- Specifically, proactive calls expand your pipeline by

  - Uncovering new leads
  - Turning leads into prospects

- They move prospects toward a proposal or quote.
- They move quotes and proposals toward a close.
- They close new business.
- They *expand* your business with existing customers.
- They build relationships in less time than any other communication pathway we can utilize.
- They make you stand out to the point of making you singular, simply because nobody else is calling.
- They make it clear that you care about your customers and prospects and that you are thinking about them.

Nothing else is this effective.

PHONE FIRST: LEAD WITH THE PHONE

The key activity in this book is making the proactive phone call (as defined above) the *first* interaction in your sales process with your customers and prospects.

Not the email inquiry without a call.

But the proactive phone call, when nothing is wrong, for the sole purpose of trying to help the person you are calling.

You can set up the call with a quick text message. That's okay.

You might even send a text or LinkedIn message in combination with a voice message, if you leave one.

But I want you to consider the proactive call the first effort in your selling process.

Before emailing.

Before sending your marketing materials.

Before dropping off your business card with the receptionist during an in-person drop-in with somebody you don't know.

Phone first, rather than waiting until you have a call scheduled much later in your selling process, perhaps to discuss a quote or negotiate.

Lead with the proactive phone call.

Call your customer or prospect and say, "Tom, it's Alex. I was thinking about you. How's your family?"

Catch up.

Connect.

Then pivot to the business:

"What are you working on these days that I can help you with?"

Only good can happen when you ask this question.

Or say, "What projects do you have coming up? I'd like to help."

This is impressive.

And memorable.

And singular.

Because nobody else is doing this.

Your call will probably be one of the only proactive calls your customer will receive this week, or this month, or even this quarter.

You will stand out, and build relationships and opportunities, very quickly this way.

That's what this book is about.

Phoning first.

PICK UP THE PHONE SUCCESS STORY

"My sales results completely changed when I started making three proactive calls every day. I mostly call customers I haven't talked to in a while. They're always happy to hear from me. And they almost always tell me what they need for that week. Then they call me back themselves to order it again."

—Marco J.; outside sales, wholesale distributor

THREE TO FIVE CALLS A DAY

Do you know how many calls three calls a day is?

Nearly 800 proactive calls over the course of a year.

Do you know how many calls five calls a day is?

Exactly 1,300 calls per year.

Let's say you have to leave messages on every one of these (which won't happen, of course). But you should expect to *usually* leave one.

I will arm you with voicemail scripts in Chapter 19 that generate return phone calls about two-thirds of the time.

That is, if you leave five voicemails per day – which takes about five minutes – you will get about 867 return calls.

And if you have a less-than-average success rate and only get half the people to return your call, that's 650 conversations with customers and prospects – building relationships and discussing opportunities for you to help them.

How can your sales not grow if you have 650 proactive conversations with people who can pay you?

That's what a *system* of proactive calling does for you, as opposed to calling only sometimes, when you happen to think of it.

We'll also examine this in the context of the other digital tools available to us and how to use them in combination with the phone – including email, LinkedIn messaging, text messaging, and video conferencing tools like Zoom.

But the secret weapon, the magic bullet, and the key to your entire *predictable* sales growth process is the phone.

Lead with the phone.

You will separate yourself from the competition.

And watch your sales grow.

CHAPTER 4

THE PHONE IS THE SINGLE MOST EFFECTIVE AND UNDERUSED SELLING TOOL WE HAVE

I n sales, the single most effective tool we have is the telephone.

It is also our most underutilized and avoided tool.

We are far more comfortable with much less effective communications like social media and email.

In this chapter, let's look at what makes the phone such a powerful tool for selling more.

And in the next chapter, we examine the reasons we avoid phone selling. Because once we understand that psychology, it becomes much easier to overcome.

REASONS THE PHONE IS THE SINGLE MOST EFFECTIVE SELLING TOOL

Phone Calls Feed the Machine

Proactive calls to customers and prospects feed your whole sales machine.

They build relationships.

They fill your calendar with appointments and meetings.

They create opportunities.

They build your pipeline.

They generate quotes and proposals.

They add on additional products and services for existing customers.

Phone calls get you the yeses very quickly. They also get you to the rejections in a hurry – which is a good thing, because we have to walk through a lot of them to get to the wins. (More on this Chapter 12.)

Proactive calls feed the machine.

Proactive calls feed your family.

You *and* Your Customers Have a Phone within Arm's Reach Almost Always

As you read this, your phone is probably within arm's reach. You probably don't even have to stand up to get it.

Because it's on your desk.

Or in your pocket.

Or in your purse.

Or maybe it's in your hand right now.

It's a tool all of us salespeople have.

There's something else, and this is kind of incredible: all of our customers have a phone within their reach, too.

At all waking, much less working, hours.

No matter what they're doing, at work or at home, this tool is with them.

Our prospects, too.

All the people who can buy from us have a phone within reach.

All the people we can help have a phone.

And almost nobody is calling it.

You Will Stand Out from the Crowd

Most salespeople assume that our customers' phones are ringing off the hook.

This is informed by our own discomfort with the phone (see the next chapter and Part 2).

The truth is, most people's phones are silent when it comes to proactive calls.

Think about your experience: When is the last time you got a call from a supplier you know, when nothing was wrong?

When is the last time somebody called you and said, "How are you? I was thinking about you. How is your family? And listen, I was wondering, what are you working on these days that I might be able to help you with? Because I'd like to help."

Can you remember the last call you got like this?

Most people say they cannot remember the last one.

But those who did receive one got it weeks or months ago. And guess what?

They remember every single aspect of that call: *who* called, *what* they wanted, *how long* the call lasted, and what each party *said* – sometimes word-for-word. They even remember what the caller's voice sounded like.

That's *amazing*, but why is this so?

Because it's the only call they've received like this in the last weeks or months.

The only one.

And they remember everything about it.

The vast majority of salespeople simply don't make proactive calls.

Which means your competition is not showing up like this.

Their customers don't get to hear their names, because they don't call.

But your customers will hear your name.

And you'll stand out from the crowd in your customers' and prospects' eyes.

Want to be totally memorable?

Make proactive phone calls to customers and prospects.

PICK UP THE PHONE SUCCESS STORY

"On at least half of the proactive calls I make, my customers tell me they are not hearing from anybody else on the phone. They tell me I am the only one doing this. It sets me apart, they say. This makes me feel good. I'm doing something others are not, and it shows in my results. My sales are up 45% this year."

—Chris O.; inside sales, manufacturer

PHONE CALLS MAKE US SINGULARLY MEMORABLE, BUT EMAIL MAKES US FORGETTABLE

If you want to be utterly forgettable, send emails instead of making calls.

If you send an email, there is a good chance you'll end up in the junk folder.

Think about that.

Your communication will be *with the trash emails.*

And even if your email gets into your recipient's inbox, you probably won't ever know it.

This is because the most common response to an email is silence.

Did your customer or prospect get your email?

You don't know.

Did they see it with their eyes?

You don't know.

Did they *read* it and process it with their brain?

No idea.

Did they make any kind of decision regarding what you emailed about?

Again, you don't know, because there was probably no response.

Interestingly, if you *don't* send the email, you have none of these problems.

Therefore, because of all the issues and questions it creates, sending an email is actually worse than doing nothing at all!

The Customer Gets to Experience That You Care

I will never suggest that you need to care more.

I think you care more than enough. Most salespeople care a great deal.

The problem is, most salespeople *care in silence.*

We don't let people know that we care.

How do you let somebody know that you care?

By showing up.

By being present.

By calling on the phone when nothing is wrong and saying, "Tom, I was thinking about you. How is your family? And what are you working on these days that I can help you with?"

When you don't make proactive calls, your customers and prospects do not think about you.

But when you *do* make proactive calls, they know you care about them.

They know you're interested in helping them (because you will actually say these words – *I'd like to help you*).

And you're probably the only one showing up like this.

And so, I am not suggesting you need to care more.

What I'm suggesting is that you *communicate* that care a little bit more.

With some proactive calls.

You Will Build Relationships in Record Time

Proactive calls supercharge relationships, especially when compared with the generally silent competition.

Proactive calls tell customers you are interested.

Proactive calls make you *present* in front of the customer.

This is impressive to your customers.

When you call, your customers will trust you faster.

They will expand their business with you faster.

Know what else will happen when you call your customers when nothing is wrong?

They will also call you.

Proactive calls generate incoming calls.

And quite frequently, these incoming calls will result in business.

Proactive Calls Take Timing Off the Table

When you reach out to customers and prospects only sometimes, when you happen to think about it, you are at the mercy of timing.

If they don't have an itch that you are offering to scratch *at the moment you call,* you will not get the business.

That's a hard way to live, because the odds of the timing of their need lining up with your rare communications are really bad.

But when you call systematically, you are constantly in your customers' minds, while your competition is not.

When you are present in their system, it takes the timing off the table.

That is, it doesn't matter *when* your customer has a need for your goods or services, because *whenever* they need something, they'll simply pick up the phone and call you.

When you are consistently present, the customer will always think of you.

It's like placing a backscratcher on your customers' and prospects' desks.

And the backscratcher has your name on it.

So when the itch comes, they pick up the only back-scratcher on their desk.

They scratch, and you get paid.

There is simply no other communications method that will generate all these benefits.

And there is certainly no other way to create these benefits *with such speed.*

You could go from an empty pipeline to one that's bursting at the seams in short order if you systematically make proactive phone calls!

WHAT ABOUT MEETINGS?

But you might be thinking, meetings are more effective than phone calls.

This is probably true.

But here's the thing about meetings: you can only have so many in a day.

A perfectly planned, very busy day might get you a handful of meetings.

You can make the same number of phone calls in less than 30 minutes.

If you get voicemail, which is more likely than not, your five calls take 5 to 10 minutes – and that's with leaving a message.

There's one more important thing: we tend to have meetings with people we know well.

Good customers, usually. Often, our very best customers.

Everyone else doesn't get to see us very often.

But phone calls take us well beyond this group.

Phone calls take us to people we don't know as well.

Which means we get to call people who are currently buying at least some products and services from our competition.

With proactive calls, we get to expand our wallet share and our market share – and the likelihood of expanding and growing our business goes way up.

Because we're communicating with people we normally would not meet with.

CHAPTER

5

WHY WE AVOID THE PHONE

If proactive calls are so singularly effective for expanding your pipeline, creating new opportunities, moving existing ones forward, cementing your relationships, and creating new business, why don't more people sell with the phone?

There are a number of reasons – both practical (not enough time) and mindset (fear of bothering or upsetting the customer). I will focus on the real-world, practical reasons in this chapter, briefly touch on the mindset issues, and dive into them in much greater detail in Part 2 of this book.

PRACTICAL REASONS WE DON'T PICK UP THE PHONE

Many of the reasons we avoid the phone are mindset- and fear-based. I will review these in the next section and Part 2.

This list is about the real-world reasons we don't make proactive calls. These are the realities of the business-to-business selling life that get in the way of our making proactive calls.

You're Very Busy – Calls and Customer Requests Come in All Day

If you've been a business-to-business salesperson for more than a year, you're very busy.

The phone rings all day long.

You're answering and reacting all day.

Answer and react.

You're serving the customer.

You have to; there's no choice.

After all, you're in the customer service business.

And you're world-class at it.

Really, who takes care of customers better than you?

They've been with you so long because you're so good at taking care of them.

Plus, when they call, you cannot say, "I'm sorry, I'm in my proactive selling window right now; please call me back when I'm being reactive again."

Customers call you on the weekends, at night, and even when you're on vacation with your family.

You take those calls.

You help your customers.

All day.

You write up quotes your customers ask for.

You reply to email, because goodness knows customers email you a lot.

Sometimes, if you manufacture or distribute something, and your customer has an urgent need, you even get in your car and drive it over to them.

Reacting to the incoming requests of your customers – and fixing their problems – keeps you incredibly busy all day.

When there is a respite, and the phone stops ringing, you sit and breathe for a minute.

You check in with your family.

You check the scores and the news (that's allowed!).

You're super crazy busy.

And it's hard to find time to do anything else.

The Good News Is: You can make five proactive calls in 15 minutes or less, so you don't need a lot of time. In fact, because you're usually going to be leaving a message, you can often move through five calls in 5 minutes. So, of course you're busy, but you have 5 to 15 minutes a day, right? Because that's all you need here.

The Customers Who Call Are Usually Upset, and Who Wants More of That?

Customers don't call you when they're happy, do they?

They rarely pick up the phone to give you positive feedback, compliments, or congratulations.

Those reasons aren't *urgent* enough to pick up the phone.

When customers call, there is almost always a problem.

Or they need something.

There is stress.

They are under pressure.

It's quite possible that somebody is yelling at them.

So what do they do?

They pick up the phone and bring that stress, pressure, and yelling to *you.*

"Here are my problems – fix them now!"

Perhaps not in those words, but that's the general feeling, right?

And so, you only talk to customers when they bring you a problem or urgency.

"You sent the wrong parts!"

"You didn't send me enough!"

"Where is it?! How do I not have this yet?!"

"I need this now! Send it immediately!" Never mind that they waited until the last possible moment to call you to make their purchase. You have to drop what you're doing and do as they ask. There isn't really a choice, is there?

This is what happens when customers call you, which takes up most of your day, day after day.

They're rarely happy.

They're usually stressed out.

There's almost always a problem.

And when you drop what you're doing to help them, they proceed to beat you up on price.

So you almost never have positive emotions when you talk to customers who call in.

So who wants to *make* proactive calls for even more negativity?

Many salespeople might think, *I've got enough angry customers hounding me already, buddy, so no thanks – I'm not going to call them so they can scream at me some more.*

This is completely understandable.

You're human.

And you want to minimize the negativity that makes up the majority of your incoming customer interactions.

> ***The Good News Is:*** The *incoming* calls are full of problems and frustrations, but you make proactive calls to customers and prospects *when nothing is wrong.* You're showing up when there isn't a problem. And, after briefly catching up, you're asking what they need help with. Their reaction will be the opposite of the emotion on your incoming calls. These customers and prospects will be grateful, pleasantly surprised, relieved, and looking for ways to thank you.

As a Result, You Don't Like the Phone

Let's review.

You're super busy.

The phone rings all day, presenting perpetual problems that must be handled immediately.

Customers who call are often frustrated, flustered, or downright angry.

And all of these reactive joys of being a salesperson come to you courtesy of . . .

The phone!

So who could blame you if your view of the phone isn't particularly positive?

And who could blame you if your instinct is to avoid using the phone?

The phone is a major source of daily work stress. It brings you anger, negativity, and condescension.

Me: "Use the phone! Make proactive calls!"

You: "No thanks, I'm good."

A few months ago, I was doing an interview with a client's salesperson.

She told me that although she has to make phone calls as part of her job, she hates the phone – to the point that when she leaves voice messages, she does not give her phone number.

Rather, she asks that people return her call with an email.

Can you believe that?

Her voicemail asks the customer to email her back!

> *The Good News Is:* The wins come quickly in this work. It doesn't take long to have a good, positive, warm, successful conversation. This will give you the energy and enthusiasm to make the next call. And the next. And suddenly, the phone will be actively making you money. It will be *predictably growing your sales.* You will find your dislike for phone calls lifting like a spent storm cloud.

You Simply Don't Have a System for Using the Phone Proactively

This is probably the simplest reason of all:

Nobody has ever armed you with a process for making proactive calls.
How do you make them?
When?
How many is enough?
Especially when the customer doesn't call back.
Who should you call?
What do you say?
What about voicemail?
What about cold calls?
What if you don't have cell phone numbers?
What about Zoom? And texting? And email?

The phone-selling books from the 1970s and 1980s don't apply to today, because now the phone is one tool in a much larger digital communication ecosystem. And as discussed in Chapter 1, it's not like there are lot of phone-selling systems and processes at your disposal.

Unless they are working with *me*, your company probably is not training you how to properly use the phone to grow your sales.

So, the most obvious reason you're not making proactive calls is that you don't have a program for doing so.

And nobody has ever taught you how.

The Good News Is: You have a system now: it's the book you're holding in your hands. The system is to make a few proactive calls a day, every day – and your sales, opportunities, and pipeline will quickly grow.

MINDSET ISSUES FOR WHY WE DON'T PICK UP THE PHONE

We will dive deeply into these issues in Part 2, but the mindset blocks that keep us from picking up the phone have one common characteristic:

They are our discomfort, not the customers'.

It is our discomfort with the phone that keeps us from making proactive calls systematically.

It is *not* the discomfort of your customers and prospects. *They want to hear from you.*

It *may* be our *projection* of our discomfort onto our customers. That is, we believe our customers don't want us to call, for all the reasons *we* do not like making calls.

Here are just some of the thoughts that keep us from picking up the phone proactively:

- I don't want to bother my customer.
- If she wants it, she'll call me, like everyone else.
- I don't want to waste their time.
- I don't want to make the customer angry or upset with me.
- If they get upset, I might *lose* the customer. And I've worked so hard to win them and then keep them.

Does this feel like thinking that's conducive to selling with the phone?

That's because it isn't.

The Good News Is: Ninety percent of salespeople, in my experience, have these thoughts and fears and discomforts. That means as soon as you can overcome these discomforts, you will instantly vault yourself into the top 10% of all salespeople.

That's why I wrote this book:

To arm you with a simple process for making proactive calls to grow your sales.

To show you that it's easy.

To show you that it doesn't take a lot of time.

To show you that your customers will be happy to hear from you, which is the opposite of what you fear.

To show you that they *want* you to call them.

And when you do it, it will give them what they want and make them happy.

You will be one of the only ones showing up for them this way.

And then they will thank you with their money.

Because they will appreciate that you care so much that you pick up the phone when nothing is wrong, and ask about their family, and ask what they need help with because you'd like to help them – they will hold on tight, and they will never let go.

You will develop one customer-for-life after another.

All of this happens when you make proactive calls, systematically, to customers and prospects.

Ready to pick up the phone and sell?

CHAPTER

6

The Phone Compared to Other Sales Communications Pathways

T he phone doesn't exist in a communications vacuum, and we have many ways to communicate with customers and prospects. Naturally, some are more effective than others; and, further, some are more *threatening* than others.

Some of these pathways make us uncomfortable.

Some do not.

Here they are, all together, positioned visually, comparing their effectiveness against the level of fear and discomfort they create.

Let's work through them in order, from most effective to least effective. We begin with the subject of this book, the proactive phone call.

Effectiveness and Threat Levels of Sales Communications Pathways

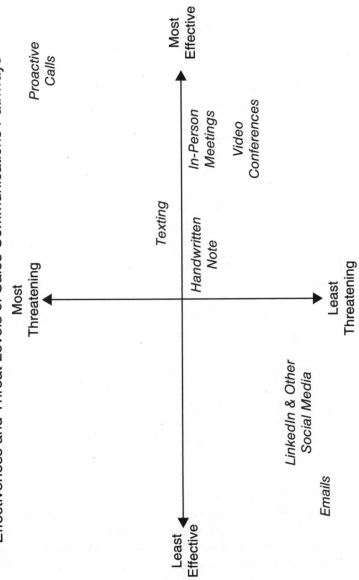

THE PROACTIVE CALL

The proactive phone call is the most effective pathway of communication a salesperson has, even more effective than the holy grail of sales advancement: the in-person meeting. This is why:

- You can make a lot more phone calls in an hour or two than you can have meetings. If you pre-plan very carefully, you can have two or three meetings in an hour or two. But you can make two or three phone calls in just a few minutes. In an hour or two, you can easily make 10 to 20 calls. Not that you have to, but for very similar effectiveness (and in many cases, *more*) than meetings, the phone requires a much lower time investment from you. This is the major advantage: using the phone, you can tell a lot more customers and prospects that you would like to help them than you can in person.

- Meetings tend to occur with your very best customers, the ones who are "big enough" or "important enough" to qualify. This is perhaps the top 5% of your customers. Maybe 10%, right? The phone gets you far beyond this group and immerses you in communications with others. Some may be very good customers who are farther away, so you don't see them much. Others may be smaller to medium-sized customers who can easily do more business with you, but because you don't meet with them, they don't think about you often. Now they will. Of course, some may be *prospects* who are not customers at all. Call them, and let them hear your name and your interest.

- Lots of salespeople try to have meetings with your customers and prospects. But very few actually pick up the phone and call when nothing is wrong. When you call a customer, you are one of the only ones doing so. It makes you memorable. For many people, it makes you singular. And even if they do not have a need at the moment you call, they will think of *you* – the one who made an effort, the one who communicated – when a need arises.

■ Phone calls do not have to be pre-scheduled; you can just call. But calls can be scheduled with a quick text message if you'd like.

So, if the phone is this powerful and effective for sales growth (x-axis), why don't we use it more? The answer was laid out in part in the previous chapter and is also covered in depth in the next part of this book.

But the short answer is that the phone is also the most threatening of all the possible communications pathways.

It is the one that induces the most fear.

It is the one that leads to the most rejection, because we can communicate with so many people so quickly.

It is the pathway that leads to the most *intimate* rejection.

On the phone, we *hear* the rejection.

Customers reject us into our ears!

Nothing else creates this kind of real discomfort: not in-person meetings (where most people either place orders or tell us they will let us know and get back to us) or video conference tools like Zoom. Text messages don't lead to verbal, personal rejection like this. And email and LinkedIn communications tend to produce silence more than anything else. (More on this below.)

The phone is the most effective communication tool we have because it lets us speak to many customers and prospects quickly. It lets us show people that we care, that we are interested, and that we are present. And it sets us apart from nearly every other salesperson who does not make proactive calls.

But we salespeople avoid the phone more than any of the tools available to us because it's the most threatening, with the highest fear factor.

In the next section, I review how to deal with this fear and overcome it so that you can leverage proactive calls to grow your sales quickly.

IN-PERSON MEETINGS

The oldest method of business communications is one of the most effective.

Everybody tries to have in-person meetings.

Your customers are extremely busy, and it's difficult for them to find the time.

And *you* are very busy. One meeting can chew up half a day.

But of course meetings are worth pursuing because it's incredibly effective to be with people face-to-face, where you can observe their body language and place of business.

And the threat level in a meeting is much lower than on the phone. The odds of rejection *during* the meeting are low, in part because the customer has agreed to see you, and in part because people don't like to say "no" to somebody who is in front of them. You've made the effort. You've traveled to the customer. They'll hold on to their rejection for later – perhaps for the phone!

I love meetings.

Nothing can take their place.

But proactive calls get us meetings, don't they?

If your goal is to get more meetings, use the phone to get you there.

I want to be clear: I will never suggest that the phone should *replace* meetings.

Rather, use proactive calling to *get* meetings.

VIDEO CONFERENCES

During the pandemic years of 2020 and 2021, video conferencing tools like Zoom took over the business communications world. On the heels of Zoom were Microsoft Teams and Cisco Webex.

Salespeople flocked to these tools.

There were a number of months where we couldn't see our customers.

So we replaced meetings with Zoom and Teams and Webex.

This was the correct thing to do.

"Thank goodness for Zoom," clients told me.

"We've pivoted," everyone said.

But we started using video conferencing in lieu of making phone calls.

In fact, people started using the two interchangeably, which is a mistake.

Replace your meetings with Zoom and Team and Webex.

But do not replace phone calls with video calls.

Why?

Because little about them is proactive.

By definition, a video conference must be scheduled.

We show up to a specific web link at a specific day and time, and we meet the customer or prospect there.

It is a previously scheduled meeting.

As a salesperson, I cannot Zoom you unexpectedly, ad hoc, and tell you I was thinking about you and that I'd like to help.

We have to put it on the calendar first.

Which is perfectly okay.

But that makes it a digital replacement for your meetings.

Think of them as *video meetings*.

Do not try to replace your proactive calls with video conferencing.

As you can see, we salespeople perceive the threat level for video conferences to be quite low. This is precisely because these sessions are previously scheduled. We know the other party will be there or, at worst, will reschedule. But there is little chance of being rejected – and there is *no chance of having to leave a voicemail!* (Which most salespeople perceive as a rejection – more on this in Part 2.)

So, video calls and meetings accomplish the same important goals in selling: we get to see our customers and prospects, read their body language, and spend some time together in person. We get to move the relationship forward and advance our sale(s) with them. Video calls and meetings are essential to the selling process.

The proactive calls in this book are designed to help you secure in-person and video meetings.

When I say that proactive calls help you feed the machine, in-person meetings are among the wonderful outcomes that they generate. Calls lead to meetings.

TEXT MESSAGES

In my experience, the importance and effectiveness of text messaging shot up during the pandemic. When we became deprived of our usual ways of interacting with our customers – particularly in person, face-to-face – the text message became a very useful pathway to fall back on.

Text messages require a few seconds to send, but their impact on moving sales toward a close is very high.

Text messages show up on the cell phones of our customers and prospects and sometimes on their computer screens. They are more far more disruptive – in a good way – than an email. If I get a text ding, I look, because it must be important.

And it's very easy and fast for the customer to respond, isn't it?

Further, there is still very little spam texting to compete with. Most texts we receive are from people we know.

You can send a text message to schedule a call. I have some clients I do not speak with on the phone without scheduling the call first via text. It's an excellent way to quickly and easily schedule your quick call: "Do you have a few minutes to connect today at 1 PM?"

You can also send a text as a follow-on to your voice messages. "Per my voicemail, I wanted to share what a client is doing for fast growth that I think would also work well for you. Is Tuesday or Wednesday good for us to connect?"

This way, you give your customer a choice: they can call you back on the phone or just text you back. You'll find most people will text back and schedule the next phone call. It's a highly effective tool to work into your proactive calling system, and one we will visit repeatedly throughout this book.

Texting is easy and comfortable for most salespeople. There is little fear of rejection or failure around texting.

Think of texting as a significant and valuable sales catalyst in your proactive calling system.

HANDWRITTEN NOTES

This is an odd entry in a chapter full of high-tech digital communications pathways, right?

If the goal is to stand out from the crowd and the competition . . .

If the goal is to tell customers and prospects we are thinking of them, and we care about them . . .

If the goal is to be memorable and impressive . . .

Few tools have a greater impact than the handwritten note!

It is the opposite of an email.

It takes a little time and effort, far more than most emails take to write.

It requires finding the mailing address and affixing some postage.

It requires a bit of thinking and planning.

And believe me when I tell you that *your* handwritten note will be the only one your customer receives this week.

And probably this month.

And this quarter.

And also this year.

The *only* drawback of a handwritten note is that it's not a two-way communication.

The customer can't talk back to you.

But, you will find, they will often *write* back to you.

Not with a handwritten note of their own, but via email.

They do not see the irony of this, but that's okay.

The next time you talk, they will probably also bring up how nice it was to receive your note.

There is no fear or threat around notes.

They take five minutes to write.

And you will be remembered as singular by your customers.

Spend a few minutes each week and send some notes – perhaps after you talk to customers and prospects on the phone!

LinkedIn and Other Social Media

Here is my general take on social media's role in sales success: If it can get you in front of your target audience, or even your target's influencers, then be there.

Since LinkedIn is the most widely used business social media, I'd like to focus this section on this space.

In general, I think most business-to-business buyers don't *make* decisions based on what they see on social media, even LinkedIn.

But using LinkedIn the right way, *in combination with other more direct communications like proactive calling, can only help us salespeople.*

What's the right way?

Two specific LinkedIn approaches are particularly useful in my experience.

First, a LinkedIn direct message is significantly more effective than an email.

This is because LinkedIn sends the recipient an email – with your name *and* LinkedIn on it.

I find that these messages get read more, and get more response, than direct emails. Especially since on LinkedIn, we are often communicating with people we don't know very well.

That said, a LinkedIn message is not nearly as effective as a text message.

The second highly effective use of LinkedIn is to spread your value there.

Assuming your connections are mostly people who can buy from you, then why not demonstrate your expertise in the form of posts and quick videos?

If you build up enough of a following and post enough value, the impact of LinkedIn becomes almost like a book you've written: your connections can access it, any time or day, and experience your significant value.

Many times, when I talk to somebody on the phone for the first time, they thank me for the value I post on LinkedIn.

I have content going up on LinkedIn every day.

What kind of material should you post?

A tip.

A suggestion.

These can be a few sentences. Often, on LinkedIn, short posts do best: a helpful article you found (with some of your own commentary), or a quick video if you're feeling like it.

Imagine a conversation with a typical customer or prospect. What would you tell them that would be helpful to them?

What *have* you said countless times that people have responded positively to, thanking you for the tip?

Post that.

Like email, there is little perceived threat or fear around posting on LinkedIn, so it's one of the less avoided pathways of communication.

EMAIL

We have arrived at the least effective and most widely utilized pathway of business development: the email.

By both measures – and, probably, *by every measure* – it is the opposite of the proactive call, which is the most effective and least used communication.

We email because it's easy, but so is the proactive call.

We email because it's really fast, but done correctly, so is the proactive call. I'll tell you how in the coming chapters.

We email because it's safe.

People won't reject us by email because they will simply not reply instead.

In fact, that's the biggest threat when it comes to emailing – the threat of no response. This is why most salespeople are far more comfortable with email than with the proactive call, where the threat is personal, verbal rejection.

We email because it makes us feel like we are making progress, like we are taking action, like we are succeeding.

But are we?

Did the email even arrive? Without a response (the usual outcome), we don't know.

Or did it get picked off by a spam filter? Is your important email in a pile with junk and trash?

Did it land in the inbox? Don't know.

Did the customer see it with their eyes? We have no idea.

If so, did she process it with her brain? No clue.

If she processed it, why hasn't she replied? We don't know.

Is she angry with you?

Did you make a mistake?

Will she ever buy from you again?

Or have you lost her forever?

We know nothing!

In fact, I believe sending an email is often worse than doing nothing at all.

Let that sink in.

Why is this my position?

Because if we *don't* send an email, we don't have any of the problems above.

We simply are where we are.

There is no fear-based perception of backward movement with this customer. No imagination-induced rejection is happening.

But sending an email and not getting a reply – which is what typically happens – can lead to all of these problems.

However, there are two "last resort" and somewhat suitable uses of email:

1. To schedule a phone call, but only when you can't text or, for some reason, can't send a direct message on LinkedIn – because those two communications are always more effective.

2. To follow up on a quote or proposal, but only if you cannot do so via phone, text, or LinkedIn message.

I hesitated even offering these as options for you, because I don't want you going to email before those other more effective pathways, but here they are.

Only if you have to.

Only if the world is ending.

Just kidding on that last one.

Sort of.

CHAPTER 7

Planners and Trackers to Help You Pick Up the Phone and Sell

Y ou can download all the tools in this chapter, and throughout the book, from my website, www.Goldfayn.com.

As we've established, the key to growing sales predictably is proactive phone calls. And the key to making calls is *knowing who to call.*

I think this is a major reason so many salespeople don't make proactive calls: we don't know who to call.

We don't spend a few minutes to make a list at the start of the week.

I also believe that although most salespeople understand the importance of following up on opportunities and quotes or proposals, we do not do so nearly enough.

Why?

Because most of us don't have an accurate record of the opportunities before us.

That's the power of the call tracker I introduce in this chapter: it will remind you of what to follow up on.

Use the three planning and tracking tools in this chapter to create a clear and powerful picture of who to proactively call and who to follow up with.

CREATE YOUR TARGET 60: A RUNNING LIST OF CUSTOMERS AND PROSPECTS YOU WANT TO COMMUNICATE WITH

The most successful salespeople who have implemented my proactive calling approach for tremendous growth keep a running list of target customers and prospects. The customers on the list can buy more – and the prospects are ideal future customers.

Here's the Target 60 Sales Success Planner you can use to lay out your own target customers and prospects:

It has only three categories of sales targets to write down:

- Top 10 prospects you have not yet talked to
- Top 20 prospects you've already talked to
- Top 30 current customers who can buy more (and what products or services to offer them)

This is 30 prospects and 30 customers.

Work from right to left. Write down the customers first, and take a shot at what else they can buy.

Then write down your prospects you've already talked to, and those you wish to make contact with.

When you complete this planner, you will have the names of 60 people to target.

Revisit it and update it monthly: advance names to the next column, from left to right; or remove names you determine no longer fit in their current column, and add new names. *This is a working list, constantly updated.* Always keep 60 current names on the planner.

Write the names of humans, not companies. We sell to humans, not companies. We build relationships with people, so write down people's names. (Of course, it's fine to include their company as well.)

What do you do once the columns are filled and the names are written?

Target 60:
Sales Success Planner

Week Of (Date):

List your top 30 customers who can buy more. Then your top 20 prospects who you've previously spoken with. And finally, your top 10 prospects you have not yet talked to but wish to make contact with.

Top 10 Prospects You Haven't Talked To	Top 20 Prospects You Have Talked To	Top 30 Cutomers Who Can Buy More (And What To Offer Them)

This tool is available as a free download at www.Goldfayn.com

© 2021 Alex Goldfayn

Call them.

Make it a priority to make three to five proactive phone calls a day to the names on your list.

Is sales growth really this simple?

Oh yes. Sustained, predictable sales growth is about making sure customers and prospects hear from us consistently when nothing is wrong.

With this planner, you will always have right in front of you the names of people you can call.

PLAN YOUR PROACTIVE CALLS FOR THE WEEK

Next, once a week, move names from the Target 60 Sales Success Planner to the Simple Proactive Call Planner. This should take 5 to 10 minutes. This planner is to be created weekly. You may carry forward names you didn't get to last week.

It's important to lay out your proactive calls for the week because the people we will call are not on our minds. They don't call us, and we don't call them because we are busy talking to the people who do call (the 10–20% who bring us problems and urgencies).

As I said earlier, I believe a major reason we do not make more proactive calls is that *we simply don't know who to call.* This is because we don't take a few minutes to think through who to call.

So take out this planner, as well as your Target 60 Sales Success Planner from this chapter. You can also utilize your contact lists, CRM, emails, texts, and voicemails to make your list for the week. Use the chapters that follow in this section to think through the kinds of customers and prospects you can lay out here.

Then keep this planner in front of you during the week.

Keep it visible.

Let it remind you who to call.

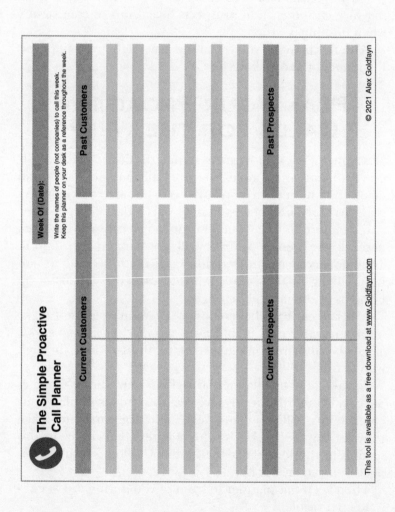

The Simple Proactive Call Planner

Week Of (Date):

Write the names of people (not companies) to call this week.
Keep this planner on your desk as a reference throughout the week.

Current Customers

Past Customers

Current Prospects

Past Prospects

This tool is available as a free download at www.Goldfayn.com

© 2021 Alex Goldfayn

FINALLY, LOG YOUR CALLS

Chapter 22 will detail why it's critical to maintain a log of your proactive calls.

	The Proactive Call Tracker		Week Of (Date):	
			Enter calls made, voicemails left, opportunities opened, opportunities progressed, and new business closed.	
Date	Customer Name & Company	Product or Services Discussed & Outcomes	$ Value	Follow-up Date & Action

This tool is available as a free download at www.Goldfayn.com   © 2021 Alex Goldfayn

This is less a log of calls than of the results and follow-up actions required.

If you don't record your calls and your progress, you will likely forget some of the opportunities you've opened and sales you've progressed with these calls.

Your day moves at a very fast pace.

Track the good stuff.

It will help your customers a great deal.

Because it will help you and your family by helping you sell more.

Download all of the planners and trackers in this book from my website: www.Goldfayn.com.

PART TWO

Your Mindset
and
Your Phone

CHAPTER

8

It's Impossible to Outsell Your Mindset

In every profession or pursuit, our mindset determines our outcomes.

That is, our behavior follows our thinking.

Henry Ford famously said, "Whether you think you can, or you think you can't, you're right."

This is a wonderful and powerful quote that I use frequently in my speeches and writing. It elegantly expresses what I believe is the key to human achievement: *our beliefs are the top drivers of our actions – and action is the only thing that leads to success.*

Another way to think about this is that it's impossible to outperform your mindset.

You will only achieve what you think you *can* achieve.

And we work in a profession that brings more rejection and failure than any other.

Nobody fails more than salespeople – not even baseball players, who fail approximately 75% of the time, on average. In sales, a success rate of just 10–20% makes us world-class.

Which means that even the best of us will get rejected all . . . day . . . long.

This is why our mindset is so important.

Sales success is about thinking the right way so we can do the right and difficult things our work requires.

SPORTS AS A PARALLEL

The annals of professional athletics are littered with supremely talented players whose mindsets and beliefs did not measure up to their world-class athletic abilities.

Many college players drafted in the first round in *every* sport – football, basketball, baseball, hockey, etc. – end up having a minimal impact on their teams. They are selected for their speed, strength, or other exceptional physical ability, and their muscles end up being far more developed than their mindsets. Often, these players who fail to meet expectations *don't believe they can.* Coaches will sometimes say that "they don't put in the work" or "they've been able to rely on talent alone until now" or, simply, " they got down on themselves." If you've ever followed sports, you've seen quotes like these.

On the other hand, players who are taken much later in their draft or are undrafted free agents often outperform their more talented and physically gifted teammates. These players tend to develop strong beliefs in their ability, and their mind is usually their strongest muscle.

The most famous example of this kind of player is Tom Brady. He was drafted in the sixth round in 2000, with a half-dozen quarterbacks selected ahead of him. Following is the draft report on Tom Brady back then. This assessment was widely agreed on by the professional scouts in the NFL, which is why every team in the league drafted multiple players that year before the guy who turned out to be the greatest and most successful player in the history of the league:

- Poor build.
- Skinny.
- Lacks great physical stature and strength.
- Gets knocked down easily.
- Lacks mobility and ability to avoid the rush.

- Lacks a really strong arm.
- Can't drive the ball downfield.
- Does not throw a really tight spiral.
- System-type player who can get exposed if forced to ad-lib.

After Brady won his seventh Super Bowl in 2021, in his first year with a new team, at the age of 42 in a league where the average age is 23, an interviewer read him some excerpts of this draft report. Here is how he responded:

"Well, that kind of gets me fired up," Brady said. "Because I'm thinking, what the hell do these people know? When people tell you, 'hey, you can't do this, or you can't do that,' and you keep overcoming that, *you build this confidence in yourself, and this belief in yourself,* that even when nobody else believes in you, that I'm still going to do it. I don't [care] what you think, because I'm going to do it. And I've *done* it."

Indeed, Tom Brady has won seven Super Bowls in his career, which is two more than any other player. But he has played in 10 of them, which may be the even more amazing statistic because the next-closest players have appeared in six.

WHY IT'S IMPOSSIBLE TO OUTSELL OUR MINDSET

You build this *confidence* in yourself, Brady says, this *belief* in yourself.

These are also two of the most important mindsets we need in order to achieve success in the sales profession. We need to pick up the phone and make the proactive calls to feed our pipeline and to feed our family.

If we are confident, we will present our value and assistance to our customers and prospects because we know we can help them.

If we believe in ourselves, we will do the uncomfortable work that sales growth requires.

If we are not confident, and if we do not believe, we simply will not make the calls that our customers want us to make and our family deserves us to make.

This is why it's impossible to outsell your mindset.

If you believe you're helping people, you make your calls.

But if you believe you're bothering people, you won't.

If you believe in your incredible value to your customers, you will call them.

If you believe you're taking their time, you won't.

Brady also said, "I'm going to do it. I've *done* it."

So have you.

You've already done it.

You've already made sales in the face of rejection.

In the face of long odds.

You've made sales that required great perseverance.

Lean from this powerful experience.

Lean on this knowledge.

You've already done it.

Now?

Simply do it again.

THE MINDSETS THAT MAKE PROACTIVE CALLING EASY

Now, let's cover the mindsets that make it easy to pick up the phone to call customers and prospects proactively.

Confidence

We've talked about confidence here, but now let's address why it is important: confident salespeople will outsell meek salespeople all day long. Who would you rather buy from, somebody who feels strongly about their ability to help you, or somebody who is timid and uncertain? Truth is, it's unlikely you will even *hear* from the meek salesperson. But the confident one will show up, be present, and try to help you.

Belief

We've already looked at believing in your great value. The opposite position is to question whether your products and services can really help your customers.

Let's go further:

I want you to believe that the customer is *lucky* when you call them because they now have an opportunity to be helped by you.

You could be calling anybody, but you picked *this* person. How lucky are they?!

When aimed inward, belief becomes *faith*. I address this in Chapter 12, which is about perseverance.

Enthusiasm

Enthusiasm is a rare commodity in the world, and, specifically, it's a key determinant of sales success. In my experience with countless sales teams, the most successful salespeople tend to be the most enthusiastic ones.

It's *possible* to be successful without enthusiasm, but it's harder.

Enthusiasm gives us the energy to overcome obstacles, failure, and rejections, all of which are central parts of the selling life.

Enthusiasm imbues us with positive energy – excitement.

The opposite of enthusiasm, then, is indifference.

And indifference will not help you make your plan for who to call each week, or pick up the phone, or continue trying even after the customer tells you no.

Positivity

Positive people are rare. This is because it's much harder work to be positive than negative.

We're surrounded by negativity – in our work, on the news, in our elections. Most opinion writers tend to take the negative position. Having worked in the media as a columnist early in my career, I know from experience that news media are *rewarded* for making you feel negative and afraid.

Did you read the news during the pandemic?

Everybody was telling us how worried and afraid we should be.

In fact, one of the major news sites had the words "apocalypse" and "apocalyptic" in its top headline for multiple days in a row.

In this reality, we must fight for our positivity.

And we must try to bring it to our customers.

Because it is rare, like a proactive call.

Like the call, positivity will make us stand out.

And it will make us memorable.

This is also very important to our selling success: like negativity, positivity is contagious. People crave it. We don't have many positive influences in our lives, and when we find them, we tend to hold on to them. If you bring customers positivity, they will grab on to you and never let go. Negativity is one of the most contagious feelings there is.

And positivity is just as contagious.

People will pay you good money for it.

Optimism

Optimism is a critical way of thinking for us salespeople.

In a profession where rejection is far more likely than success, optimism will get you through to the next call and the next success.

When you are optimistic, you believe success is possible on the next call and, potentially, on every call.

When you are pessimistic, you believe rejection is likely – that no matter how hard you try or how much time you spend, you won't succeed.

When you are optimistic, you believe you will figure out how to help this customer, no matter what they need.

When you are pessimistic, you feel you will be let down.

Optimists tend to have an internal locus of control: we believe it is up to us to do the work for sales success. It is within our control to grow our sales. It is up to us.

Pessimists place responsibility for their success outwardly: the company sets the price too high; the company hasn't given them the right product mix; colleagues let them down in the delivery of what they sell.

Pessimists blame, but optimists take action.

Pessimists experience failure as something that happens to them, but optimists see success as something they create.

Who would you rather buy from: an optimist or a pessimist?

Who do you think outperforms the other?

Gratitude

Countless studies find that grateful professionals outperform those who lack gratitude.

What is gratitude?

In my opinion, it is the *conscious appreciation of what we have and also what we do not have.*

Here's what gratitude does for us salespeople:

We can be grateful that we get to call customers and prospects to try to help them.

Or we can resent this activity because we know we are likely to be rejected.

We can feel gratitude for our rejections because they bring us closer to the next success.

Or we can wallow in the rejection and experience negative thoughts like, "Of *course* they said no, everyone does." This kind of thinking is toxic to the work we do as salespeople, and yet it's very common.

What is there to be grateful for?

- Our customers who trust us.

- Our prospects we can help.

- That people we know will take our call and be happy to talk to us.

- That we have an incredible selling tool like the phone at our disposal: it lets us call people, and text them, and email them, and write them on LinkedIn, and even video conference with them. All on a single device – wirelessly – from wherever we are. That's amazing! (You can *feel* the difference between this mindset and the one that dreads and avoids the phone because of the rejection it may bring. Right?!)

- We can be grateful for the sales we win.
- And the sales we progress.
- And even our rejections, because they bring us closer to the next yes. (More on this in Chapter 12.)

THESE MINDSETS GO TOGETHER

The mindsets laid out in this chapter are inclusive of each other. That is, people who are confident also tend to believe strongly in their value. And they are also usually enthusiastic, positive, optimistic, and grateful.

Similarly, people who are meek tend to not have a strong understanding of their value. They also tend to be apathetic, negative, and pessimistic.

In this business, we need the mindset that will help us do our work: pick up the phone proactively, fight through obstacles, overcome rejection, and deal with failure.

Without this, there will be no success in sales.

Now that we've reviewed the mindsets that proactive calling requires, I want to emphasize two critical items.

OUR MINDSET IS NEITHER FIXED NOR PERMANENT – YOU CAN DEVELOP IT

If you are not confident today, you can become that way.

I did.

I was not always confident.

But a combination of client success and personal willpower brought me to confidence.

How do *you* develop confidence?

Think back to your customer successes.

Think about how you are available at all times to your customers. They can call you at night, or on the weekend, or while you're *on vacation,* and you do what is necessary to help them.

Think about how you bend over backward to get your customers what they need, *when* they need it. If necessary, you get in your own car and bring the product to your customers.

Take confidence from these experiences.

Think about how many customers have been with you for a long time.

There's a reason for this: they are confident in you.

You should be confident in you, too.

Your customers value you.

You should have an unflinching belief in your value.

If somebody gets angry at you for trying to help them, that's *their* problem, not yours. We'll explore this much further in the coming chapters.

You can do some thinking work right now – write it down if it's easier – to lay out proof of your immense value.

Think about all the good you do.

Believe it.

Believe *in* it.

Believe in yourself.

Behave accordingly.

YOU DEVELOP THESE MINDSETS SIMPLY BY CHOOSING TO DO SO

How do you develop your confidence, belief, and other mindsets detailed here?

You *decide* to do so.

You decide you will be confident and then do the mental work to become so.

You decide to be enthusiastic and look for opportunities to bring that energy to your customers.

You decide to be positive and grateful and happy – and then get going by focusing on developing these mindsets.

You see, we human beings are lucky.

We get to *choose* to move through our days.

We're the only ones who get to choose.

Animals don't get a choice.

Plants don't get a choice.

But we do.

We get to decide.

Whether you think you can, or you think you can't, you're right.

Which will you decide to think?

It's completely up to you.

The choice is entirely yours.

I would suggest that "thinking you can" will help your customers more.

In turn, "thinking you can" will help you sell more.

And "thinking you can" will bring home more money to your family.

Which is exactly what your customers, and you, and your family deserve.

So, what will you decide?

It's a pretty easy choice, right?

CHAPTER

9

FEAR IS
THE ENEMY
OF PICKING
UP THE
PHONE

If confidence, belief, positivity, enthusiasm, optimism, and gratitude are the mindsets that enable sales success and make it easy to make proactive calls, what gets in the way? Which mindset is so prevalent and so overpowering that it controls the behavior of nearly all salespeople?

The answer is a single ugly word.

It's damaging and harmful, and it costs us money.

It hurts our customers and our families.

This word, this mindset, is *fear*.

Fear is the most powerful human emotion because it totally controls our behavior.

It stops us from doing what we know is right and good.

Nearly all salespeople know, for example, that proactive phone calls are a more effective way to grow sales than emails, and yet most people email instead of call.

Nearly all salespeople know that following up on quotes and proposals will close more of them, and yet we don't call.

Nearly all salespeople know that asking for referrals is a great way to expand our customer base, and yet we tend not to ask.

We *think* about these efforts a lot. We even think about doing them.

We may even *plan* how and when we will take these actions.

But then, most times, we don't do them.

We find other things to do. Safer things that make us less uncomfortable.

Or we replan our plan. We try to make it perfect, but it will never be all the way perfect.

It is fear that does this to us.

In fact, if you find yourself avoiding something that you know you should be doing, it is almost always because of fear.

Trying to lose a few pounds, but putting off that diet?

It's probably because you're afraid of missing out on the foods and drinks you enjoy. I know for a fact that this is *my* issue in this area.

What about the exercise program you might be delaying?

It's probably because you have a fear of the effort that will be required and the discomfort it may cause.

ON FEAR IN SALES

How does this work in sales?

What do *we* fear as salespeople?

Almost always, ours is a *fear of rejection.*

We are totally afraid of being told no, and we'll do anything to avoid it.

This fact informs nearly everything we do.

Why are most salespeople exceptional at taking orders and serving customers? *Because there is little fear around these activities.* They are deemed safe. Solve the problem, and the customer will be happy.

Why do most salespeople much prefer face-to-face visits, or even Zoom video calls, to phone calls?

Because the customer is expecting you.

These activities are scheduled in advance.

There is little risk of personal rejection.

On the phone, the opposite is true:

The odds of what most salespeople perceive as "failure" are very high. Here is what usually happens when you call a customer proactively:

- They won't pick up.
- They will pick up and say no. The odds of getting a yes are very low on a call-by-call basis.
- You will have to leave a message.

Most salespeople perceive each of these things as an intense personal failure. But look again at this short list.

Are these things really failures?

If the customer doesn't pick up, have you failed? Have they rejected you? They were simply *busy*, which has nothing to do with us. But we experience it personally, as a failure.

If the customer does pick up, and you speak, and they say no, have you really failed? No: you didn't get the order *this one time*. You've failed at nothing. In fact, *you've succeeded* by trying. You've succeeded at showing the customer you care. You've succeeded because the customer heard your name, and your company name, and your effort and enthusiasm. As a result, the next time the customer needs something that you provide, they will be more likely to think of you.

Doesn't sound like failure or rejection, does it?

Finally, most people perceive leaving a voicemail as a personal rejection from the customer. Again, this is our own bias at work. In reality, when you leave a message, the customer gets to hear from *you*. The competition didn't leave a voicemail; *you did*. This puts you at a great advantage. It puts you in the front of that customer's mind, and even if they don't return *this* call, they'll be calling you the next time a need comes up.

FEARS ARE NOT GROUNDED IN REALITY

Our fear keeps us from picking up the phone, but our fears are not rational.

What we are afraid of (rejection) is not what actually happens.

In your head, the outcome of making proactive calls can be damaging and terrible.

We perceive that the customer is screaming at us.

We imagine them being very angry with us.

We fear losing the customer forever.

In reality, consider the chances of *any* of these things happening when we call a customer to say, "I was thinking about you. How's your family? What are you working on these days that I can help with?"

The chances are incredibly low.

I've taught more than 10,000 salespeople these approaches to sales growth, and I've not yet heard of a single instance in which a customer got angry after being told the salesperson would like to help them.

Here are some other reasons we feel fear around picking up the phone:

- We salespeople get rejected all day long as it is, and making proactive calls voluntarily places us closer to even more rejection. "Here I am," we announce to the people we call. "Reject me!" Who wants to get more rejection like this? Of course, as you'll read in the next chapter, a lot of things we perceive as rejection or failure – like having to leave a voicemail – are not rejection at all. Rather, they are an opportunity.

- The odds of success are very low, but the odds of failure are very high. So why would we go into a situation like this voluntarily?

- Most salespeople assume that calling customers and prospects means making cold calls, and we hate cold calls. Most of the calls we *receive* are cold calls. Most people are no good at making them, and it's terrible to talk to these folks. So we hate the cold-calling experience, and we want to avoid it. But, as discussed, most of the proactive calls laid out in this book go to people who know you or recognize your name or your company name. All calls are not cold calls, but in our fearful mind, we often make it so.

- We equate calling people on the phone with junk calls and even junk emails. We get a lot of both, right? Pre-recorded nonsense and email spam from strangers who want to partner with us and make us millions. We don't want to be those people, and we certainly don't want to be perceived like those people. Let me assure you: the proactive calls that this book is about are relationship calls with people you know. They are calls with people you are trying to help, and those people *want* more of your help. By making your proactive calls, you will be separating yourself from the people making junk calls and sending spam. This is the opposite of that.

- It's uncomfortable to call somebody who is not expecting us.

- For most people, even salespeople, it is unnatural. We don't do it much. We don't *receive* a lot of proactive calls from our own suppliers. So we have little practice with this activity.

- We perceive phone calls as dangerous. And biologically, our fight-or-flight brains seek to escape danger. This is why most salespeople are so adept at phone avoidance.

Our fears around the phone are *biological!*

SO, WHAT DO WE DO ABOUT THIS FEAR?

If avoiding the phone is one of the strongest instincts we have as salespeople, but the phone is so important to our success, how do we deal with this fear? What do we do about it?

First, realize it. Understand that you are avoiding the phone because of your fear around it. This sounds absurdly obvious, but many times the fear happens so quickly – in microseconds, and in our subconscious – that we don't even know it's there. It is what's called *an automatic fear*. It happens without us thinking about it. So, as with most self-growth, the first step is awareness, and now you have it.

Second, understand that all of the things we imagine happening are highly unlikely to occur:

- You will probably not get screamed at.

- The customer will probably not fire you if you show up to help them.

- Leaving a voice message is an opportunity to advance your sale, which is the opposite of a failure.

Third, realize that the *worst* that can happen is not so bad. As my 12-year-old son Noah says, "Dad, the worst that can happen is a one-word answer."

That's the worst that can happen: the customer will say no.

Or the customer will be silent, and we will be able to follow up.

But there is *no* scenario in which you will proactively call somebody and your life will be at risk, which is equal to the danger our automatic fears make us feel when we *think* about picking up the phone. Nobody will shoot at us, as an old business mentor of ours used to say.

Here are the four possibilities that are most likely to happen:

1. We will have a nice conversation and open up a new opportunity.

2. Or the customer will tell us they don't need *that*, but can we help them with *this*.

3. Or they will say they're in good shape now, but thanks for checking in.

4. Or we will leave a voicemail.

These four outcomes cover about 98% of what will occur when you pick up the phone.

Fourth, in practical behavioral terms, simply make the first proactive call. I'll cover this in depth in Chapter 13.

For now, you know exactly what is probably keeping you from making calls – and also other important activities you might be avoiding. And in the next chapter, one at a time, I'll disarm the specific fears and discomforts we salespeople have with telephone selling.

CHAPTER

10

LET'S TALK ABOUT OUR SPECIFIC FEARS AROUND PHONE SELLING

Now you know which mindsets are helpful for picking up the phone and being systematically present for customers and prospects. We've also established that fear of rejection and failure is the biggest reason we avoid doing so. In this chapter, I'd like to look at the specific fears and discomforts that make it difficult for us salespeople to go to the phone and call customers and prospects.

For each item, I'll lay out the fear, which is almost always worse in our minds than in reality, with potential consequences far worse than reality – and then I'll compare it to how customers *actually* see your effort. We'll look at the fear versus the reality.

This way, when you're feeling one of these resistances to picking up the phone, simply flip to this chapter and read the "reality" that matches your fear.

REMEMBER THAT YOU'RE MOSTLY CALLING PEOPLE YOU KNOW

One more important setup item before we dive into these fears: remember that the idea is to call people you know first and foremost. The odds are very high that you know hundreds of customers and prospects you are not regularly talking with on the phone. These are the most ideal people to call proactively because they know your name, and you know theirs. *You've interacted before.*

After you've called everyone in this group of people, you can call people who recognize your company name, if not your own name. Perhaps they dealt with somebody else at your organization. Maybe they're on autopilot, buying from your company only when they initiate it. Most companies have *many* customers like this, far more than the customers who interact with salespeople on a regular basis. Or maybe they simply buy from a competitor, and they know your company but have never interacted with anyone before. (There are a lot of people like this in your world, right?)

And after you've called everybody in these two groups (again, *hundreds* of people) and you've communicated systematically with all of them, then, if it's impossible to avoid, you can start talking to people you don't know. But you can warm these calls up dramatically by *referencing customers you work with who these folks would recognize.* This way, it's a room-temperature call, at least. More on this in Chapter 35.

As you read about these fears, I'd like you to be thinking about proactive calls as going to people you know. People you've talked to before, probably. If not, people who have done business with your company. And as a worst case, people you do not know but who would recognize the company names of some of your other customers. *These are not cold cold calls.*

THE FEAR: I DON'T WANT TO BE SEEN AS A USED CAR SALESPERSON.

Used car salespeople call unannounced, our fear tells us.

Used car salespeople are sleazy. And manipulative. And hated. Nobody likes them.

Used car salespeople are the *worst*. They give all salespeople a bad name. They make us all look bad.

You don't want to be perceived that way.

Rightfully so.

Nobody does.

The Reality: Your customers and prospects want to hear from you, and they appreciate it.

Remember, in this effort, you're usually calling people you know – and more than anyone else, you're calling your happy customers.

They will not perceive you as sleazy or manipulative.

They will see you as helpful.

And caring.

And present.

Tell somebody you'd like to help them more, and nobody will ever tell you they don't want to be helped.

A "used car salesperson" is a cartoon in our head.

It's a dirty character from a bad book or movie.

You are the opposite of a used car salesperson.

You are helpful, interested, and considerate.

Customers will be the opposite of angry or frustrated when you contact them.

They will be grateful.

They will look for ways to thank you.

Usually, they will do so with their business.

THE FEAR: I DON'T WANT TO BOTHER THE CUSTOMER.

Your customers are busy.

They have enough problems. They don't need another one.

Plus, whenever you talk to them, they sound really busy, always in a hurry.

You don't want to be yet another bother for the customer.

The reality: You are not bothering them – you are helping them.

Always remember that when you call, you are doing so with a helpful heart and helpful intentions.

First, you're likely calling somebody you know, or who knows you or at least your company.

When you follow the scripts in Part 4 and 5, you are literally asking the customer, "What are you working on that I can help with? Because I'd like to help. That way, you won't have to think about it again later. Let me take that off your desk."

What an incredible kindness you are doing for this customer. You are saving them time! They won't have to worry about this issue once they place this order with you. This is an incredible gift to give somebody. By showing up and being present, you are releasing them from future worry about the product or service you are going to help them with. *You are doing them a favor!*

Most people don't have anyone in their lives like this.

So, *you* be that person.

The customer will feel grateful for the opportunity to buy from you.

THE FEAR: THEIR PHONE IS ALREADY RINGING OFF THE HOOK.

This is a very common concern for people who sell: everybody is calling them. Their phone never stops ringing.

I don't want to be yet another annoying call. I don't want to be that person.

The Reality: Almost nobody is calling proactively.

This widely held misconception hurts many salespeople, their families, their employers, and their customers.

Does *your* phone ring a lot?

Do *you* get a lot of calls from salespeople or suppliers you know when nothing is wrong?

Do you hear from salespeople who ask about your family and your kids, and then ask what you're working on because they'd like to help?

We *think* our customers' phones are ringing off the hook, but the truth is, their phones are just like our phones.

Our customers' phones are generally silent when it comes to proactive calls.

They probably get some junk calls.

They probably get problem calls with lots of issues to react to and work on and fix.

We get a lot of those calls too, right?

Because that's generally the only kind of person who calls – the person with the problem or urgency.

But who calls when nothing is wrong?

Who calls to check on you, to make sure you're good?

That's right.

Almost nobody does that.

But, now, you will.

And you will be one of the only ones.

And as a result, you will instantly vault yourself into the top 5% of salespeople.

The Fear: If they want to talk to me, they'll call me.

People call me all day long; they're the ones who want to talk.

It's true – people call all day.

They place orders that need to be delivered immediately.

Or they submit problems that must be resolved.

These are the people who call – the squeaky wheels. The problem bringers. The urgent demanders.

You spend much of the day talking with them and helping them, but they make up just 10–20% of your customers.

The Reality: Most of your happy customers are not calling you, and they are on autopilot.

It *feels* like people are calling you all day, but you're only talking to a small subset of your customers. Outside of the small group of customers who bring you problems and urgencies, few others call you on the phone.

Satisfied, happy customers are not calling.

They email their orders.

Or they place them on your website.

They take delivery and order again.

But nobody from your company is really talking to them.

Nobody is building relationships with them.

Nobody is asking them what else they might need or what they have coming up.

They are on auto-pilot with your company.

They are your best and happiest customers, returning on their own, order after order, year after year.

But they are generally untethered to anyone in sales.

Almost tragically, by default, they are house accounts.

But why don't they call? They're frequent repeat buys – what keeps them from picking up the phone and calling you, as the others do?

Two major reasons:

1. They're simply creatures of habit, and they are not used to interacting with you this way. Through your lack of proactive communication, these customers have been taught that this is not how to buy from you.

2. They are the squeaky wheels for *other* suppliers. Believe me, they are calling people with problems and urgencies who are not serving them as well as you do.

So imagine how pleased they will be when you reach out to them.

Imagine how grateful they will feel when you tell them you'd like to help them more. What are they buying from your competition, which is obviously not as good as you, that *you* can help them with?

Because you'd like to help them more.

This will be a rare and amazing experience for them.

And they will be happy to thank you with their money.

THE FEAR: I DO NOT ENJOY GETTING PHONE CALLS, SO PEOPLE OBVIOUSLY DO NOT *LIKE* TO TALK ON THE PHONE.

If you don't like to get phone calls, you are far from alone.

Phone calls are usually junk.

They're often pre-recorded.

Sometimes they're scams. ("This is the IRS. You must return our call immediately." Right . . .)

If they aren't these things, they're cold calls, with that annoying pause between when we answer the phone and when the caller talks.

After the painful pause, they say, "Hello?" like they are surprised we're on the phone!

These are people we do not know.

Sometimes they're from another country.

These calls are lazy crap.

It's no wonder we hate them.

The Reality: Calls from helpful, prepared providers are nearly non-existent.

You will probably be the only person who calls the customer proactively today.

You may be one of the only people to call them when nothing is wrong.

You will probably be the only person they know who calls and doesn't bring them a problem.

As a result, they will be very pleasantly surprised about your call.

They may answer expecting a problem. They may be tense at the "Hello," because they expect a problem to fly at them. It almost always does.

They may even say something like, "What's wrong, did something happen?"

But when they realize you're not bringing them an urgent problem, they will relax.

You will have a nice conversation.

You will ask what they have coming up that you can help with.

They will *thank* you for calling.

They will appreciate you.

Only you.

Not the competition.

Because the competition is not calling.

THE FEAR: NOBODY ANSWERS THEIR PHONE ANYWAY, SO WHY BOTHER?

I always get voicemail, so what's the point of even trying to call?
Also, if I don't recognize the number, I don't pick up.

It's true: most calls go to voicemail.

Even calls to people you know.

Even with customers who are currently buying from you.

And if somebody doesn't recognize your number, they let it go to voicemail, just as you and I do.

So, if you're going to get voicemail every single time, why call?

Why try?

Why not just email?

The Reality: Voicemails tell your customers you care, and many will lead to return calls.

Yes, most calls will go to voicemail.

So what?

Go to the scripts in Chapter 19, and leave your message.

Then send a text or LinkedIn message to give your customer a choice of how to get back to you.

You will find that two-thirds of the people you connect with will call you back.

Again, these are calls to people who know you, or know *of* you, or at least know of your company.

But something else happens, which is a fantastic benefit to our sales work: the customer you leave a message for hears your name.

And your company name.

And they get to experience that you tried.

You made an effort.

You were thinking of them.

That's incredibly valuable to them, and to you.

Even if you don't talk.

Even if you get voicemail.

Remember, the competition won't be doing this.

They won't be calling, and they won't be leaving a message.

But you will.

And guess who will get the business when the time comes to award it?

My money is on you!

A FINAL NOTE ON FEAR – THESE ARE *OUR* DISCOMFORTS

What do these specific fears have common?

They are our discomforts.

These are salespeople's issues.

The customer does not feel them.

The customer *wants* to know you called.

They *want* to hear from you.

Nobody calls them, so they *appreciate* it when you check in and tell them that helping them is important to you.

They are dealing with problems and urgencies all day.

A call from you when nothing is wrong will be a welcome reprieve from their troubles.

When we allow our fears to prevent us from calling them, we keep our great value from them.

We *hurt them.*

We force them toward the competition, which they do not want.

They want to buy from you.

They appreciate buying from you.

Don't let your fears – which make you imagine a reality that's the opposite of what the customer wants from you – keep you from helping your customers.

You have immense value to your customers.

Share it generously.

And enjoy all the sales that result.

CHAPTER

11

Believe in Your Value as Much as Your Customers Do

One critically important path for overcoming your fears is to realize how much your customers value you.

They've been with you for years for a reason.

They keep coming back to you because you take great care of them.

If you asked what they like best about working with you, here is what they would say:

You're always available.

You're far more reachable and responsive than the competition. You even get back to your customers on weekends and in the evening.

You save your customers time because they can simply call, text, or email you, and you take care of it right away.

You make sure they get their product or service delivered on time, or even early.

As a result of saving them time, your customers get to focus on other priorities, which they would not otherwise have time for. As a result, you make them more productive.

And they even become more profitable because of you, because there's much less wasted time with you.

They get to do what they promised to their own customers, who, in turn, keep coming back to them.

With other suppliers – your competition – they have to follow up a lot. They have to check on the status of their orders. They wonder whether they will be able to service *their* customers, because this depends on receiving your products or services on time.

As a result, other suppliers require much more of your customers' time than you do.

Working with you helps your customers look good to *their* customers.

And you also help them look good to their bosses.

Some of them will even say that working with your company makes it *possible* for them to be in business.

You fight for your customers.

You bend over backward for them.

How do I know this?

Because I've interviewed thousands of my client's happy customers over the years as a part of my revenue growth projects, and this is what they tell me.

These customers are not the ones calling you daily with problems or issues.

Rather, they are among the 80–90% of your customers who are happy and quiet.

They are not the squeaky wheels.

They are the satisfied ones.

When I go to them, I ask them what they like best about working with you.

And these are things that they talk about.

They describe what a pleasure it is to work with you.

Frequently, they will say you are their friend.

That you know each other's spouses.

That you've had meals together, or golfed or hunted together.

They will say that they know you are always there for them.

They know this.

Do you?

They appreciate your great value and can quickly describe it to anyone who asks.

Do *you* know you're great?

Draw confidence from these successes.

Draw confidence from all the value you bring to your customers.

Your customers have confidence in you because of this.

Now I'm asking *you* to share their confidence in you.

I'm asking you to understand that your competition is not this good.

Others are not as good as you.

I know this.

And your customers know this.

So, really, what the hell is there to be afraid of?

PROACTIVE CALLING SUCCESS STORY

I was speaking with a distributor's customer on the phone, as I do for every revenue growth project, and here is what the customer said about his salesperson, Trevor:

> *Trevor is a hound dog, and I'm that way, too. He's always checking in with me. If we said we were going to talk in two days, and we haven't connected, he's there, man. He's calling me to make sure we're on track.*

Me: And this is a good thing?

Customer: *Oh yeah, oh yeah. He's here. He cares. And that's really something. A lot of people aren't like that.*

Me: So it doesn't bother you that he's proactive with you on the phone?

Customer: *It's exactly the opposite. He's trying to make sure I'm good.*

Me, to you now:

What more proof do you need about the power of proactive calls?

CHAPTER

12

PERSEVERANCE IS A SALES SUPERPOWER

The single most important mindset you can develop for selling success – and, probably, all of life – is perseverance.

For salespeople, perseverance is a superpower.

Perseverance is a mindset *and* a behavior, and it can improve nearly every area of our selling work.

THE DEFINITION OF PERSEVERANCE

For our purposes, a good definition of *perseverance* in sales is **to continue to try to help customers in the midst of failure or rejection.**

Let's look at the components of this definition:

To continue to try means to keep going. Keep working. Keep making multiple efforts.

To help customers is a very important way to think about what we do as salespeople. Think of your work as helping, because that is what you're doing. This small mindset shift makes it easier not only to persevere but also to do our work.

In the midst of failure or rejection means we have to keep doing the right things even when they are not succeeding. In fact, we must continue to try *during* failure and rejection.

Why is perseverance such an effective tool in our work?

Because more than anything else, our work is defined by dealing with rejection and overcoming it.

OURS IS A REJECTION PROFESSION

And, by necessary extension, success in sales demands that we apply perseverance in our thinking and our actions to overcome rejection.

Nobody Gets Rejected More Than Salespeople

In baseball, you go to the Hall of Fame if you fail 70% of the time. A .300 hitter is among the best in the game.

In sales, we fail *more* than that.

In fact, a 10–20% success rate in business-to-business sales is among the very best in the business.

Which means nobody fails more than us.

Nobody gets told no more than us.

Nobody gets ghosted more than us.

People go silent and stop communicating with us all the time.

Every day, if you're doing it right.

The Rejections Get Us to the Wins

But the noes get us to the yeses.

The rejections lead to the wins.

The failures bring the successes.

We must experience and get through the failures to attain any semblance of success in our work.

If a salesperson averages a 10% success rate, then that person knows it takes nine failures to get to the one success, and the counter starts again.

So instead of experiencing each rejection negatively, dramatically, as the end of the world – nine times over – it's a lot easier to simply tell yourself that you are now one rejection closer to your sale.

I came across a fabulous Winston Churchill quote recently. He said, "Success is going from failure to failure without losing your enthusiasm."

Welcome to sales, right?

Going from failure to failure is *literally* what we do every day.

We talked about enthusiasm in Chapter 8.

Churchill says success comes from staying enthusiastic *while we fail over and over* because success follows failure.

More accurately, success requires failures.

You will not succeed at anything interesting or compelling (like attaining a good sale) without failing a lot.

So, fail with enthusiasm.

It will take you to the next effort.

SALES SUCCESS IS LIKE A RARE AND VALUABLE ROOKIE CARD

Success is a rare and valuable rookie card in a pack of otherwise common and uninteresting cards.

How do we get to the desirable cards?

We have to get through a bunch of boring, plain, and uninteresting common cards. (Failure is also all those things, isn't it? It's boring, common, plain, and uninteresting.)

We have to keep opening packs. Each pack, like each call, is an opportunity to succeed.

So go through the packs, and the calls, and explore your opportunities.

With enthusiasm.

PERSEVERANCE IS TWICE AS IMPORTANT AS TALENT OR TECHNIQUE

Research from the field of positive psychology finds that perseverance is twice as important for success as talent is.

That is, not giving up and continuing to fight is twice as important as how good you are.

This means perseverance is two-thirds of the equation to success, while talent and technique are one-third.

It doesn't matter how good you are if you give up at the first failure or rejection.

This is why less talented people are frequently more successful than their more gifted colleagues or teammates.

In these cases, the less talented people have developed more grit and perseverance, quite probably *because* they are less naturally gifted. They've learned to rely on their effort and persistence instead of on their abilities.

Make perseverance your core mindset and your key behavior trait in sales.

It will get you through most challenges and most difficult times.

Develop your perseverance, and then learn to rely on it.

It's a selling superpower.

THE NEXT EFFORT MAY BE THE ONE THAT GETS IT DONE

What will get you from one failure to the next?

What will make you keep trying?

Perseverance in your mind, in your heart, and in your actions.

Bring on the rejections!

Each one means you're closer to the successes.

Thomas Edison said, "Many of life's failures are people who did not realize how close they were to success when they gave up."

Isn't that wonderful?

You never know if the next action will be the one that leads to success, so why would you stop?

My speaking audiences have heard me tell this story: in my consulting practice, a few years ago, I had a prospect who had attended one of my speeches.

He asked me to follow up with him about the possibility of working together and left me his contact info.

The next week, I called the number, and the guy who picked up the phone told me "He's not here" and took a message.

I didn't get a return call, so I called again.

And again.

The same person answered the phone each time and took the messages.

On the fifth attempt, the same guy said to me, "Maybe if he doesn't return this call, don't call back."

I immediately answered, "I'll talk to you tomorrow."

I called the next day, and sure enough, I got the owner.

We talked several times and, wouldn't you know it, he became a client.

When I was training his people how to sell more, guess who was in the audience? The guy who told me not to call back!

I stood *right* next to him – uncomfortably close – and told this very story about him (anonymously – only he and I knew who I was talking about).

I took offense at his suggestion.

I make a living by persevering and helping my clients.

He, apparently, makes a living by answering phones and telling people how to do their jobs.

His boss asked me to try to help him. (This is how I think of prospect inquiries, which I find useful; I think you may also benefit from thinking this way.)

Most people aren't good at perseverance.

They don't get many opportunities to practice and develop their perseverance muscle.

But we salespeople do, goodness knows.

Ironically, the people who are good at perseverance are the ones who appreciate it when others around them apply it! When salespeople call me and don't give up, I try to reward them with business or at least referrals. This is what you will find with your customers: they will appreciate your efforts and look for ways to thank you for your attempts to help them.

If I had stopped at the fourth or fifth effort, I never would have known that the next attempt would have been the one that would lead to the conversation.

Also, if you've failed, say, seven times already, then what is an eighth failure, really?

What's the difference between seven failures and eight?

I would suggest there's no difference.

You had no sale, and you still have no sale.

So try again.

Unless the customer *tells* you to stop trying – at which point you immediately honor their request – your job is to try to keep helping them.

Your customer deserves for you you keep trying.

Your family deserves for you to keep trying.

So keep going.

Even when there's no hope.

Keep going anyway.

Because *this next effort* may be the one that changes everything, forever.

And if you don't make this effort, you will never know!

PERSEVERANCE EVEN WHEN IT FEELS HOPELESS

Dale Carnegie said, "Most of the important things in the world have been accomplished by people who have kept on trying when there seemed no hope at all."

The most successful salespeople I know are the ones who never give up, no matter how difficult the situation is.

I attribute my business success to my perseverance more than anything else.

I've been in business my entire working life – I've never had a job and never received a paycheck every two weeks from an employer, as nice as that might seem sometimes.

Although I run a thriving consultancy – I don't know of a larger solo consulting company – my business has had many struggles over the years.

As a result, my wife and I have been all the way out of money multiple times in our lives.

Luckily, that was a long time ago, but there were some terribly difficult years when I was learning and figuring out how business, marketing, writing, speaking, selling, and delivering work.

There were times when my wife believed in my work and future success far more than I did.

Even then, when it felt hopeless, I persevered.

Nothing was working.

No matter what I tried, or how hard, success wouldn't come.

For years at a time.

And then, like a switch that flipped, success started happening.

I sold a project.

And then another one.

And another.

During the hard times, I felt like I was beating my head against an invisible but painful wall.

These difficult stretches were easily the toughest professional moments of my life.

But they also *built* the most toughness.

You can't develop grit unless there are difficulties to battle through.

And in sales, goodness knows, we have difficulties, rejections, and failures daily. So there is no shortage of opportunities to practice our perseverance!

In sales, perseverance will bring you through even the darkest times.

Because it's darkest before the dawn.

Don't give up in the darkness.

Apply your perseverance in the darkness.

And you will dramatically accelerate the coming of the dawn.

HAVE FAITH IN YOURSELF AND THE PROCESS

There is another important component in the perseverance discussion for us salespeople:

Faith.

Not religious faith, but faith in yourself.

Faith in continuing to do the right things (proactive calling, for example) even when they aren't working.

Even when you're not experiencing success.

Knowing you are doing the right things that will eventually bring success will be critical in helping you to continue taking action.

Believe that you are doing the right thing, even if there isn't success at this moment.

As you read this right now, you know proactive calls to customers and prospects are incredibly effective for growing your sales.

You can think back to specific sales phone calls you've had that have opened new opportunities, or progressed them, or closed new sales.

You've succeeded with phone calls in ways that email or other communications simply cannot replicate.

You know this now.

Develop your faith in doing the right things from these past successes.

And believe in this truth when you're making your calls, doing all the right things, and not seeing the kind of success you'd like.

Let your faith in the process get you through.

What is the process?

Proactively calling three to five customers or prospects you know, when nothing is wrong, every day.

Do this, and you will grow.

Perhaps not with every call.

But working this simple system will bring success.

Have faith.

TWO KINDS OF PERSEVERANCE

There are two kinds of perseverance: micro-perseverance and macro-perseverance.

Micro-perseverance is applied to individual sales opportunities, where the customer does not answer her phone or return your call or respond to your quote or proposal. This is perseverance during your calls. Micro-perseverance is continuing to take action to move the individual sale forward. It is trying again or trying a different way when the customer says no. It is following up even when the sale feels unlikely, because you will show this customer that you care.

Macro-perseverance zooms out from the individual sale and focuses on your overall selling work. It is continuing to make your calls, even when you feel that maybe you don't have it in you. Macro-perseverance is applied between the calls, and at the start of your day, or in bed when you are alone with your thoughts. It is determining to continue to try and to fight even when you might feel like curling up into a defensive posture. It is doing the work and making the effort when success has been rare lately.

Because it is precisely the work and the effort that will bring success back.

You'll need to develop and apply both micro- and macro-perseverance to attain the kind of sales success you deserve.

The Critical Importance of Multiple Efforts

Most sales require multiple efforts – even with existing happy customers.

You have to start the conversation and open the opportunity.

You may have to discuss the opportunity again for it to take shape.

Then you'll send a quote.

And then you may need to follow up on the quote.

Sometimes, more than once.

And then you'll have to ask for the business multiple times.

So, as you can see, even a relatively easy sale may require perseverance over an extended period of time.

Who Deserves for Us to Persevere?

We often stop trying or persevering with certain customers because we feel the sale is unlikely. We stop calling because we fear they no longer want us to.

In reality, these customers *want* us to keep trying to help them. Unless they've told you specifically to stop trying to help them (and this happens rarely to never), you should continue to try to help them.

Why?

Because your customers deserve for you to persevere.

Here is the list of people who deserve your perseverance, beginning with current customers:

Your current customers: They get tremendous value from your work. They appreciate your work. You are available to them, while most of the competition is not. You save them time. They trust you. *You help them more than the competition does.* They've also been there for you. They've

supported you with their business and helped you provide for your family. They deserve for you to not give up
and to keep trying to help them. Pick up the phone and
ask them what else they need, because you'd like to help
them more.

Your past customers: These poor people are suffering
through the competition right now. They are struggling.
They went away from you, perhaps because they were
offered a lower price, and they're *paying* the price for
that decision now. Products and services have not been
delivered accurately or timely by the competition. Things
have taken a significant turn for the worse. Try again with
them. Call them. Tell them you miss them and you'd like
to help them again.

Your prospective customers: Your prospects have never
experienced your value. They've never been lucky enough
to be helped by you. And they deserve to, don't they?
Life would be a lot better with you than with the competition. So if we do this selling work to help people, which I
believe – and working with *you* would help these prospects
so much – then persevere and make multiple efforts to
help your prospects.

Your family: We spend more time at work than we do with
our family. They support us. They fight for us. And when
we don't give up and persevere, we are fighting for them.
They deserve this from us. We owe them this. In my family, as I described earlier in this chapter, without the support of my wife – without her lifting me up when I was
down because of all the rejection and failure – I would
never have gotten through that difficult period. I certainly wouldn't have the trust in my perseverance that I
do now. And my business absolutely would not be where
it is now. She deserves for me to keep trying, keep going,
even when I don't want to, even when I don't feel like
it. Your family does, too. Your family deserves the additional income your perseverance creates and all the good
things it can buy.

Your co-workers: All the people at your organization deserve for you to continue implementing micro- and macro-perseverance. Your fellow salespeople will look to you as an example of what perseverance can accomplish. The ownership or top leadership of your company will benefit from the business growth you create. And all the other employees who are in roles that directly or indirectly produce or deliver what you sell – think they'll be happy if you don't give up? You doing your job allows them to *have* a job!

AND, AT THE TOP OF THE LIST OF THOSE WHO DESERVE FOR YOU TO APPLY PERSEVERANCE TO YOUR SELLING WORK: YOU!

You deserve all the success that comes from your perseverance.

You deserve the additional take-home money.

You deserve the company growth you will create for your firm.

You deserve the job security that comes along with that.

You deserve the *options* you will create for yourself and your family as a result of the growing sales your perseverance will lead to.

You deserve the customer success and happiness that will come your way.

You work incredibly hard.

Apply perseverance, and enjoy the exponential results that occur.

You deserve them.

CHAPTER

13

THE FIRST PHONE CALL IS THE ANSWER!

The chapter is for you if:

- You find yourself stuck in the reactive circle, where customers are calling with problems and urgencies for you to address all day long.

- You're wondering how to start developing optimism, enthusiasm, gratitude, and positivity.

- You're not sure how to pick up the phone because your fear of rejection is getting in the way.

- Most importantly, you're not sure how to move yourself into the righteous circle of making proactive calls, offering to help people more, and growing your sales.

The answer for all of the above is – *the first phone call.*

JUST MAKE THE FIRST PROACTIVE CALL.

Call a customer or prospect you haven't talked to in a while.
Call a "friendly."
This is a person you know.
Somebody who will be happy to hear from you.

Somebody you will have a nice conversation with.

You will talk about family, life, and work.

And then you will ask them, "What are you working on these days that I can help you with? Because I'd like to help."

And they will tell you all about their headaches and what they have coming up.

You will have a good conversation.

You will connect with somebody who is pleased to talk with you.

You will catch up, and pour cement on your relationship.

You will uncover opportunities you can help this customer with.

This will give you energy.

And positivity.

And you will also find enthusiasm.

You'll feel good.

And you can leverage this energy, positivity, enthusiasm, and good feeling to make the next call.

You see?

Proactive calls beget proactive calls.

The more you call, the more you will want to call.

It will become addicting, in a good way.

You will want more of the connection.

More of the relationship building.

And best of all, more of the sales growth.

Because you will be rewarded for your efforts not only with positivity, enthusiasm, and good feelings – you will also be rewarded with these customers' additional business.

They will reward you with their money.

Do you see a downside here?

There isn't one, is there?

The first call is the answer.

It will bring you the mindsets that will facilitate additional calls.

And it will break you out of the reactive vicious circle – where fear and trepidation rule the day – and move you firmly into the proactive righteous circle, where confidence and optimism reign.

That's where you want to be.

Life is better there.
Business is better there.
You deserve to be there.
Go there.
The first phone call is the answer.

PICK UP THE PHONE
SUCCESS STORY

"I have to tell you, since your training, I make three proactive calls every morning, and it has really changed how I do my job. First of all, the customers are happy to hear from me, and I get to talk to nice people. Second, I used to just email everybody, and it was all a numbers game. I just tried to email as many people as I could. I was anxious and frustrated all the time. Now, I'm actually enjoying my job. I have nice conversations. I get to hear in people's tone of voice that I'm really helping them. It has made me look forward to getting out of bed every day!"

—Angie C.; inside salesperson,
wholesale product distributor

PART THREE

CALL TACTICS, MECHANICS, AND STRATEGIES

CHAPTER

14

How Proactive Calls Can Fit into Your Sales Process

Now that we've discussed the importance of your mindset and thinking, addressed how debilitating fear of rejection and failure can be, and looked at the sales superpower of perseverance, we shift now to *action*.

Starting with this chapter, the rest of this book is about the behaviors that will grow your sales quickly and dramatically.

This chapter covers the great benefits that proactive calling can create in your sales process. Shortly, we will look at *who* you can call, and how calling customers and prospects can jam your pipeline full of opportunities and move them along toward a close – and beyond.

There aren't scripts for what to say in this chapter – those are coming up in Parts 4 and 5.

Rather, this chapter looks at *where* you can utilize the proactive call in your sales process and the immense benefits you will create when you do so.

Before we begin, I want to point out that for *all* of the incredibly valuable outcomes below, the proactive phone call is superior to any other kind of communication.

In many cases, it isn't even clear what the second-best option is. You're not going to have face-to-face meetings very often to build relationships with prospects or follow up on quotes or proposals. You may have some, but as we discussed previously, how many meetings can you really have in a day? About as many as you can call in a few minutes throughout the day.

Is email the second-best option? Perhaps for some things – like quote and proposal follow-ups – but it's such a distant second that you can't even see it with binoculars.

WHAT PROACTIVE CALLS CAN DO FOR YOU

Here are the results and benefits that proactive calling can create for you. Let's look at them on a basic business-to-business sales pipeline:

BUILDING RELATIONSHIPS WITH PROSPECTS BEFORE YOUR SALES CONVERSATION BEGINS

You can call prospects you know, and those you do not know. This pre-sale part of your pipeline is the only time you will call people you do not know. If you think about it, you've talked to a lot of people who did not buy from you.

Or people who buy somewhere else, currently. Or even people who used to buy from you but stopped. This past customer would be listed in this group.

But if you really want to call prospects you don't know yet – or perhaps if you *need* to, as part of your job – call customers who would recognize your name or at least your company's name. Any familiarity is better than no familiarity, and I'm suggesting that even when it comes to people who are not yet buying from you, you know a lot of them.

With these prospects, lead with the phone.

Get to know them.

Ask about their work.

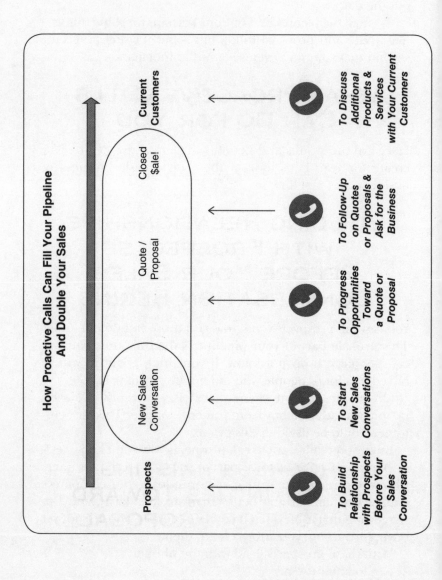

How Proactive Calls Can Fill Your Pipeline And Double Your Sales

Prospects | New Sales Conversation | Quote / Proposal | Closed $ale! | Current Customers

To Build Relationship with Prospects Before Your Sales Conversation

To Start New Sales Conversations

To Progress Opportunities Toward a Quote or Proposal

To Follow-Up on Quotes or Proposals & Ask for the Business

To Discuss Additional Products & Services with Your Current Customers

And tell them about yours.

Learn about their family and their job priorities.

You don't even have to take the conversation to business, because that will come up on its own.

Your purpose here is to set up or schedule the next call, which will become the first discussion in your sales conversation.

START NEW SALES CONVERSATIONS WITH NEW PROSPECTS

These are calls that kick off your selling process.

You will discuss what you do for other customers like them, and what their situation and needs are.

You'll ask a lot of questions and mostly listen (see Chapter 21, which is about silence).

There is no better tool for beginning the sales conversation than the phone.

In second place, in terms of effectiveness for starting sales conversations, is the video call. But that needs to be scheduled. There's no Zooming somebody unannounced – they have to meet you there. As a result, you can't leave a message on Zoom. I love that with the phone, you can demonstrate to your prospect that you are thinking about them and that they are important to you. *You can say that,* without scheduling anything in advance, directly to the person or on a voice message.

PROGRESS EXISTING OPPORTUNITIES TOWARD A QUOTE OR PROPOSAL

From the first sales conversation, getting the business becomes a series of follow-ups.

Always schedule the next interaction before you end the current interaction. The ensuing proactive calls will work to moving your opportunity toward a quote or proposal.

Your calls will do the work of making the customer comfortable with your product or services.

These efforts will lay the foundation for a long-term relationship and multiple purchases across many years.

But first, we need the initial quote or proposal.

Follow Up on Quotes and Proposals to Close Them

The proactive call is incredibly effective as a follow-up to your quotes and proposals.

Even in a voice message, you can tell the customer that you're thinking about them and wondering if they need anything else on that quote.

You can tell them you'd like to help them.

You can tell them this work is important to you.

They will be able to hear this in your voice.

Customers want you to follow up with them.

It shows them you are interested and you care.

And you will be the only one following up like this.

It's easy to rise above the competition.

Begin Discussions about Additional Products or Services for Your Existing Customers

For most business-to-business salespeople, this is the best-paying proactive call.

Selling more to your existing customers is how you can make the most money, the fastest.

Especially if you sell products.

Because right now, as you read this, your customers are buying things from *you*, and they're buying other things from the competition.

They *could* buy those other things from you.

They *need* these things.

But they buy them elsewhere because they niche you for the products they buy from you, and they niche the other guys for those other products.

Worse, *we niche our customers.*

If they need it, we think, they'll ask us for it.

Well, they can't ask us, because they don't think about us for those products.

And they may not even know they can buy those products from us.

So this step is about asking the customer what else they buy.

And what else they need.

And what they need quoted.

And what projects they have coming up.

And guess what will happen when you ask them?

They will *tell* you.

Because they want to be helped more.

By you.

This is what proactive calls can do for you.

NOTE: YOU KNOW THESE PEOPLE

For four-and-a-half out of five of these points on your pipeline, you *know* the people you are calling. The half is for the prospects you do not yet know, since with our approach, you *will* know about half the prospects you call.

Proactive phone calls should be made to people we know first and foremost.

Make proactive calls to friendlies.

They will be happy to hear from you!

Pick Up the Phone
Success Story

"The thing that surprised me the most with making these proactive calls is how happy my customers are to tell me what they need. I thought they would keep it more to themselves, but what you say is exactly right: people just want some help. And when I call and ask how I can help, they tell me several ways on the spot. And it usually involves them buying something from me."

—Marcus G.; outside salesperson, manufacturer

CHAPTER

15

Pre- and Post-Call Communi- cations

We begin with some basic guidelines for how to make your proactive calls.

PHONE FIRST: MAKE CALLS THE FIRST COMMUNICATION IN YOUR SELLING WORK

Make the phone call your first communication in each of the sale situations detailed in the last chapter.

Even before emailing (if you email at all), calling first is effective because almost nobody else does it. If you make your phone call the tip of your communications spear, you will be a sales rarity for all the people you call – and totally singular for many of them.

You will stand out from nearly everyone your customers and prospects deal with, and that's a tremendous benefit in our profession. Your customers and prospects will be shocked and amazed that somebody cared enough to pick up the phone and communicate with them.

Make your proactive calls the tip of your selling spear – the first effort in each of the pipeline situations detailed here. Before long, you will find your sales growing accordingly.

THE OPTIONAL PRE-CALL COMMUNICATION

If you know the customer well enough that you are comfortable sending a pre-call text message, and you prefer to schedule the call so the customer is expecting you, do so.

YOUR PRE-CALL COMMUNICATION

Here is an example of a text message you can send before your proactive call:

> "Greg, it's Alex Goldfayn; hope you're doing great. Would love to catch up and get your take on something. Do you have a few minutes this afternoon or tomorrow for a quick call?"

Keep these texts short and to the point.

What do you want their take on? Other products or services you can help with. Or what else they need quoted. Or what projects they have coming up.

End with the question, or ask, so they can reply quickly.

I'd send a text because an email is useful here only if you know the person very well (that's who will typically reply to an email). *But you're already talking to customers you know very well, so the value of the proactive call is somewhat diminished.* Also, because most emails go unanswered, and your proactive calls – which are positive, enthusiastic, and rare expressions of caring for and helping your customers – are now negatively affected by the black hole that is email. Sometimes the people you know best will reply to your emails, *but you're already talking to these people.*

Send a text first if you'd like the customer to expect your call.

But understand that when you do so, you're taking some of the "proactive" surprise impact out of your effort. I think you should do it if it will help you make your calls, but I'm also absolutely firm on the fact that you should not call *only* those who reply to a text message.

Remember the purpose of this outreach:

To be present.
To try to help.

This should not be dependent on a returned electronic communication.

SEND A POST-CALL COMMUNICATION

After you call, as a rule, whether you spoke or left a message, send another electronic communication.

This one should also be a text message if possible. If not, go with a LinkedIn message as a second option; and if you can't send that, go with email.

YOUR POST-CALL COMMUNICATION AFTER LEAVING A VOICEMAIL

"Greg, it's Alex Goldfayn. Per my voicemail, I'd like to catch up and get your take on something. What's a good day for us to speak this week?"

Or:

"Greg, it's Alex Goldfayn. Per my voicemail, I have a customer similar to you doing some interesting things with us that I think would work really well for you. Would love to tell you about it, because I think it'd help you. Do you have a few minutes to talk on Tuesday or Wednesday?"

These communications are fast and easy to reply to.

And, most importantly, they give your customers and prospects a choice about how to get back to you.

If it's convenient, they'll call you back.

If it's more convenient, they'll send you a text or LinkedIn message or email.

But now they have options about how to go about getting back to you.

And if you follow these methods about leading with the phone and sending a post-call communication, you should expect half or more of your customers to get back to you.

YOUR POST-CALL COMMUNICATION IF YOU TALKED WITH YOUR CUSTOMER OR PROSPECT

If you spoke and secured a next communication or action – which should be the goal of *every* communication – you can send this follow-up communication:

> "Greg, it was great talking with you. I enjoyed it a lot and look forward to our next conversation on [the day/date] at [the time]."

Send a calendar invite if you decided to take it to email.

You're just confirming what you both agreed to.

Send a confirmation email the day before your next scheduled conversation.

PICK UP THE PHONE SUCCESS STORY

"I always send a text before I call, to schedule it, and almost everybody gets back to me with a day and time to do so. They know I'm not calling to bother them and that I'm actually going to help them.

"I also text after my voicemails like you recommend, and 90% of my clients get back to me by text, not with a call. But that's fine, they're in touch, and we get the business!"

—Wilson R.; client sales,
equipment service contractor

CHAPTER

WHAT TIME OF DAY SHOULD YOU CALL?

T he thing about work-days is that the later it gets, the busier *they* get.

Schedules rarely open up as the hours go by.

Customer requests and service needs and problems to resolve and hoops to jump through only pile up as the day goes on.

So what is the best time to make your three to five proactive calls per day?

Before those demands and issues begin to come in.

The best time to make your proactive calls is first thing in the morning.

When you have the most energy.

When you have the clearest mind.

When you are most rested.

When you are best able to overcome your own discomfort.

Do the uncomfortable work first thing in the morning. That's when it is easiest to get done.

It's like exercising:

I know that if I don't get on the treadmill or bike first thing in the morning, before I start working, it's probably not going to happen that day. Because work is super busy with a full calendar, and then I have a drink with my wife, and then that's it. That drink is the workout eliminator.

Just as your appointments and daily responsibilities are the proactive call killers.

One salesperson who implements my recommendations to call her customers and prospects systematically described this morning calling time as *sacrosanct.*

Here is our conversation about this:

Me: What if you get busy?

Her: I do it anyway.

Me: What if you don't feel like it?

Her: I still make my calls. Every morning, I make my calls.

Me: How do you do that?

Her: **It's the most important thing I do.** *That time is sacrosanct.*

Me: Why is it so important?

Her: Because it's very fast, and it sets up my day positively. I've done the hard thing. Everything else today will be easier. And it grows my pipeline and my sales. I can't think of anything that's more important.

There you go.

For a salesperson, these sales calls are the most important thing you will do in your work.

And that morning time is, indeed, sacrosanct.

You will dramatically grow your sales, help countless customers, contribute to growing your company, and feed your family in those first few morning minutes of the day.

EAT THE FROG

Mark Twain said, "If it's your job to eat a frog, it's best to do it first thing in the morning."

I love this quote.

Eating a frog is unpleasant.

It won't taste great unless properly prepared, and who has time first thing in the morning to cook a frog correctly?

So do the most unpleasant thing first.

When you have the focus and energy to overcome your own resistance and avoidance.

Mark Twain also said, "If it's your job to eat two frogs, it's best to eat the biggest one first."

This means if you're making three to five proactive calls in a morning, make the most uncomfortable call first.

Call the person you are most fearful about.

Arrange your calls in order from most difficult to easiest, pick up your phone, and go.

Makes sense, right?

Who knew that Mark Twain knew so much about sales calls?!

CHAPTER

17

How Many Calls Per Day?

Salespeople often tell me they don't have time to make proactive calls.

They say they're too busy.

After all, customer calls are incoming constantly, right?

These customers have needs, requests, and – as we've already established, more than anything else – problems. Customers bring us problems and urgencies.

If they need product, they need it, like, *now*.

So who has time to make a lot of proactive calls?

Here's the thing: using our approach, it doesn't take that many proactive calls to make a huge impact on your business.

If you were to make 3 proactive calls a day, you would be making 780 calls a year.

What about 5 calls a day?

That is 1,300 proactive calls a year.

Do you know how long it takes to make three to five proactive calls a day?

Most days, it takes just three to five minutes. And that includes sending a follow-up text or LinkedIn note and logging your call (writing it down) in your Proactive Call Tracker.

That's it.

Why is it so fast?

Because usually, you'll be leaving a voicemail – a highly effective, well-rehearsed voicemail from one of our scripts in Chapter 19.

Now, let's assume you're calling people you know – or at least people who recognize your name or your company's name. If you leave one of our voicemails and follow up with a text message or LinkedIn note as laid out in this book, you should expect approximately two-thirds of these people to communicate back to you. Let's be conservative and make it "only" a 50% return communication rate.

So, if you make 3 calls a day, which is 780 total calls annually, you should expect to have 390 proactive customer and prospect communications over the course of a full year. Do you think that's enough to grow your sales significantly?

I would guess that it is, because remember, these are proactive calls where you and the customer or prospect are intentionally discussing ways you can help.

THREE PROACTIVE CALLS DAILY IS ENOUGH TO DRIVE UP YOUR SALES SIGNIFICANTLY

But if you need more calls, go to four or five a day.

If you make five proactive calls a day, or 1,300 a year, with a conservative average of a 50% return communication rate, you will enjoy 750 new interactions annually with people who can pay you.

And you will create these 750 interactions, on most days, in five minutes per day, because that's how long it will take you to make three to five calls, leave a message, and follow up with a text or email or LinkedIn note.

Sound like a good use of your time? I agree!

SO, HOW MANY CALLS PER DAY IS THE RIGHT NUMBER?

Start with three to five calls a day.

You pick, and adjust from there.

Give it two weeks, see how the rhythm feels, and edit your number as you go.

Now let's pick up the phone and sell.

PICK UP THE PHONE SUCCESS STORY

"I work in a showroom, and our customers are mostly retail customers. But I've made it a point to call them after they buy something to check to see if everything is going well with their new products. They are so amazed when I call them and frequently tell me that they can't remember the last time they got a phone call like this. This makes me feel good, and it makes them think of me the next time they need something."

—Jamie P.; salesperson, retail

CHAPTER

18

THE POWER OF A POMODORO TIMER

So we've honed in on doing three to five proactive calls per day, first thing in the morning. We've discussed how these fast and easy efforts add up for dramatic results.

Let me give you another tool to help you get your calling done: a pomodoro timer. *Pomodoro* is the Italian word for tomato, so it's not a surprise that the pomodoro timer originated as a kitchen timer in the shape of a tomato. You'd turn the top half (of the plastic tomato!), and it would tick down to zero and then ding.

Well, the productivity folks adopted the concept into the digital world. For our purposes, a pomodoro timer is a simple app you can download onto your computer, tablet, or smartphone. Certain apps have a version for each of those platforms, and if you get the paid version, the timer continues seamlessly from one device to the next. That is, you can start the timer on your computer and walk away with your phone, and the timer will automatically continue there.

WHY USE A POMODORO TIMER?

I've found a pomodoro timer very effective for various parts of my work, especially for making calls.

Why? Because sometimes, when you have an undefined window of time, it's hard to start something important that isn't urgent.

Proactive calls are easy to avoid:

> This is because, by their very definition, proactive calls are not urgent (but they are very important to your sales success).

> Instead of making calls, we'll browse the Internet, check the news, look at last night's scores, do a little shopping, research our next vacation, text our friends, or pretty much anything else.

> *The timer brings urgency, which makes it easier to start making your proactive calls.*

HOW TO USE IT

Set your pomodoro timer to 5 or 10 minutes. That's all this takes.

Yes, even five minutes is enough to make three calls and send three texts or LinkedIn follow-ups, because you're probably going to leave a voicemail (so plan for that). And if your customer or prospect picks up the phone, you have a happy surprise and a nice, positive conversation.

See how fast and easy this really important effort is, which you have been avoiding? Set your timer, start your timer.

As long as the clock is running, make your calls. When the clock stops running, take a break.

Another great benefit of using a pomodoro timer is that you can set your break intervals as well. For example, I write for 25 minutes at a time. If the clock is running, I am writing. When the 25 minutes is up, the timer automatically switches to 5 minutes, and that's my break time. I refill my coffee, talk to my wife, or do that shopping! When break time is over, the timer dings at me, and I'm back to work for another 25 minutes.

I know I can plow through two or three such intervals every day. And when my book deadlines approach, I do two-a-days – one round of two or three in the mornings and another in the afternoons.

Use the same process for your calls: 5 to 10 minutes, the timer runs, you make your calls. Five-minute break, do something fun. Then, if you're feeling like it, do another round of 5 to 10 minutes.

You'll be amazed at how quickly and easily you will plow through your proactive calls this way. Because really, what's 5 or 10 minutes? You'll blink, and it will be over.

A pomodoro timer helps bring structure and a bit of urgency to the very important selling work of making proactive calls. Use it as a catalyst in your process.

PICK UP THE PHONE SUCCESS STORY

"I just closed a big order, and I really had to work for this one. It probably took five phone calls and follow-ups to get this business. If I had stopped calling after one or two or three calls, I would not have gotten this business. It took many calls, but they were all quick calls. I actually got the business when the customer finally called me back. He didn't return the first four calls, but on the last one, for some reason, he called me back. It just reminded me of the importance of staying in front of my customers."

—Thomas S.; inside salesperson, distributor

CHAPTER

19

Always Leave a Voicemail: Simple Scripts to Get Your Calls Returned

I f you make a lot of calls, you'll get a lot of voicemail.

In fact, one of the most frequent questions I get is, *should I leave a message?*

Not long ago, in the middle of the pandemic, I ran an interesting poll on LinkedIn about this.

The question I asked was, "Should salespeople leave voicemails on their sales calls?"

The poll was open for 24 hours and had nearly 10,000 views and 663 responses.

Nearly 70% voted yes. Which means 207 salespeople said, *no,* don't leave a message.

Presumably, this means that *they* do not leave messages when calling.

I find this fascinating.

If you don't leave a voicemail, how will people know you even called?

How will they know you *tried?*

How will people know you care?

How will people know you can help them?

How will they know you want to help them?

They won't, if you don't leave a message.

They *can't* know.

Because even though you made the effort, they cannot experience it.

If you don't leave a message, it's like you did nothing.

When you don't leave messages, your customers simply experience silence.

They don't know you're trying to help them, even though you are.

They can't buy from you, even if they want to.

Don't put people who need your help in this position.

Don't put yourself in this position.

You don't deserve it.

And your customer doesn't deserve the silence.

They deserve your help.

They deserve to know you tried to help them.

Leave a message.

The answer is yes.

Every single time.

Because you should plan to get your customers' and prospects' voicemail about 80% of the time, you should plan to leave a message.

As everyone who has called a customer or prospect knows, voicemail is the likely outcome for the vast majority of our calls.

This is usually because the customer is busy and not expecting your call. Setting up your calls quickly with a text message will help a great deal with this.

COMPONENTS OF AN EFFECTIVE VOICE MESSAGE

A good voicemail has the following components:

- State their name and your name. Let them know who's calling.

- Tell them you hope they're doing well, and their family also. Family is the most important thing to most people. It certainly is to me, and probably to you too. Family is why we work, right? Family is why we struggle and persevere. So make sure to mention that you hope their family is doing well.

■ Tell the customer or prospect you were thinking about them. Always let the person you are calling know you are thinking about them. This is flattering, and you honor them by doing so. It makes the recipient feel good.

■ Tell them *why* you were thinking about them. What reminded you of them? Another customer? A conversation or interaction you had? A product or service you recently sold? This is an important connection you get to make with the person you are calling. You bring them closer to you by explaining why you thought of them.

■ Explain that you'd like to tell them more. You're just planting the seed when you tell them what made you think of them. And then, say you'd like to tell them more about this. You have more details to share.

■ State that you think they'll find it useful or valuable. This will pique their interest, which is important because ultimately, people just want to be helped. And you can help them.

■ Also let them know that you want to catch up and hear about their latest news or developments. This adds the personal, or human, element.

■ State your phone number clearly, and repeat it. I have to write this here because, oddly, I've received voice-mails without a number. Or, many times, people will state their number just once, and the connection is unclear, and the number doesn't come across. Repeat the number twice to avoid this possibility.

■ Make it clear you only need a few minutes. Let them know they won't need a half-hour or hour to call you. You just need a few minutes.

While this seems like a lot of components, you can leave this message very quickly, as you'll see below.

Here's the first version, which takes exactly 18 seconds to leave if you speak at a medium, relaxed pace. I timed it.

YOUR VOICEMAIL SCRIPT IF YOU'RE CALLING SOMEBODY YOU KNOW: OPTION 1

"Joe, it's Alex Goldfayn. Hope you and your family are doing well. I was just thinking about you because I was working with a client who reminded me of you. They're buying some products from us that are doing really well for them and I think would work great for you, too. I'd love to tell you about it and, of course, catch up and hear about what's happening in your world. Here's my number; please call if you have a few minutes. I'll send a quick text [or LinkedIn message, or email] as well if it's easier for you to schedule a time to talk that way. Thanks, Joe!"

Again, this message takes 18 seconds.

The best voice messages are fast.

Don't get into too much detail.

Just tell the customer why you called, why you were thinking about them, and that you'd like to catch up. And tell them how to call you. That's it.

YOUR VOICEMAIL SCRIPT IF YOU'RE CALLING SOMEBODY YOU KNOW: OPTION 2

"Mike, it's Alex Goldfayn. Hope you and your family are doing great. I was thinking about you because I have some new products here that I think would work really well for you and your customers. I'd love to tell you about them because I think you'll find these items useful. I'd also enjoy catching up and hearing what's happening in your world. Here's my number – please give me a ring if you have a few minutes. I'll send a quick text [or LinkedIn message, or email] as well if it's easier for you to schedule a time to talk that way. Thanks, Mike!"

This message also takes 18 seconds to leave.

It follows the same approach: identify yourself, say you hope their family is well, tell them you were thinking about them and why, tell them you'd also enjoy catching up, state your number twice, and tell them you only require a few minutes. Done.

Now let's look at a voicemail for somebody you don't know.

A Voicemail Script for Somebody You Don't Know: Option 1

"Hi Joe, it's Alex Goldfayn. I hope you and your family are doing well. This is Alex Goldfayn, with the Revenue Growth Consultancy. I work with customers like X and Y in your industry [name two companies that this person will recognize], and they're averaging 10–20% annual sales growth with me. I think some of the same approaches would work well for you also. Would love to tell you about it, if you have a few minutes. Please give me a call on my cell at this number if you have a few minutes. [Repeat twice]. I'll send a quick text [or LinkedIn message, or email] as well if it's easier for you to schedule a time to talk that way. Thank you."

Twenty seconds for this one.

It follows the same model, with the key difference being that you name two customers they would recognize, and you mention the products or services those customers are buying from you – which you believe would also be of interest to this prospect. This shows you've thought things through before you picked up the phone. It shows you did your research about this prospect, and you have some specific high-value details you'd like to share.

A VOICEMAIL SCRIPT FOR SOMEBODY YOU DON'T KNOW: OPTION 2

"Hi Chris, it's Alex Goldfayn with the Revenue Growth Consultancy. I hope you are doing well and your family is also. Listen, I was talking with my customer Paul Manning the other day, and your name came up. I wanted to reach out and tell you about the exciting work we're doing for Paul – he's up 20% in new sales over last year. I think many of the same approaches would work well for you also. Please give me a call at this number if you have a few minutes. I'll send a quick text [or LinkedIn message, or email] as well if it's easier for you to schedule a time to talk that way. Thanks, Chris."

Eighteen seconds.

This voicemail also mentions the name of a mutual contact – your customer, and the prospect's peer. The prospect hears your name and your customer's name (which he or she recognizes) and that you have some helpful details that are working well for the person he or she knows.

That's a pretty good reason to pick up the phone and call you back.

Send an Electronic Message After Leaving Your Voicemail

After every voicemail, send an electronic message.

This gives your customer or prospect a choice in how to get back to you.

They can pick the telephone, but most of them will select the electronic communication.

Remember, we're looking to schedule a call, not play phone tag.

So an electronic message is highly effective for this purpose, and they will usually select that option to get back to you with a time or two that work for them.

At this point, the decision becomes not whether to return your call or not. Rather, it is *should I call back or text back?*

In order of effectiveness, here are the tools to use:

1. *A text message* is far and away the most effective kind of electronic communication and totally ideal for setting up a time to speak. This is because it comes to the home screen of your contact's phone. It also probably dings audibly. And it might vibrate their smartwatch. This is highly noticeable and is certain to be seen by your customer or prospect. If you have a cell phone, send the text. If they don't want you to, they'll tell you. But if they've shared their cell number – either directly, or on their card, or in their email signature – you should not hesitate to use both the voice *and* text functionality. A text message is a completely legitimate form of communication these days.

2. *A LinkedIn message* will be much less effective than a text but much more productive than sending an email. It will still likely land in your contact's email program like Outlook, but it is more likely to be seen than an email. People pay more attention to a message from the LinkedIn platform due to all of the

meaning connected to it – networking, potential job opportunities, etc.

3. *An email* is the least likely to be seen for all of the reasons covered earlier in this book. It is the most likely to land you in the spam and junk folders, with the other trash. And that's not where you want to be.

To summarize this important chapter:

Always leave a message so the customer knows you called.
So the customer knows you tried.
So the customer knows you care.
Make your message quick and also about something that is helpful to the customer.
Send a text or electronic communication after each voicemail.
So with this approach, every voicemail has two steps: the message you speak, and the message you type, ideally with your thumbs.
Leave your voicemails, and enjoy the influx of return communications, opportunities, and resulting quotes and proposals.
And most importantly, enjoy all the sales growth you will generate!

CHAPTER

20

An Effective Proactive Call Has Three Parts

A successful proactive call has three main parts:

1. The opening, where you spend a few minutes building your relationship

2. The shift to business, where you ask some specific questions

3. The pivot to the sale or the next communication

ALTOGETHER, EACH OF THESE CALLS LASTS 5 TO 10 MINUTES – NO MORE

They're very fast and highly effective. Let's go through each portion of a proactive call now.

Part One: The Opening

Here is where you say hello, catch up, and lay the foundation for the rest of your call.

Focus on the other person, and ask about their family and their kids if applicable.

LANGUAGE IF YOU KNOW THE CUSTOMER OR PROSPECT

"Joe, it's Alex Goldfayn. How are you? I was thinking about you. How's your family? Kids doing well? How has their school year been?"

Language If This Is Your First Interaction

"Hi Joe, it's Alex Goldfayn with the Revenue Growth Consultancy. I was referred to you by my friend and customer John Anderson from XYZ Company. How are you?"

or . . .

"Hi Joe, it's Alex Goldfayn with the Revenue Growth Consultancy. I was working with a client similar to you, and they were having excellent success with a few processes [or products] of mine, and I wanted to pick up the phone and tell you about it because I think it can be helpful for you, too. Do you have a couple of minutes?

"How are you? All good with your family? How is everybody getting through this past year?"

Regardless of the option you select, these openings are quick: a sentence or two.

Always ask about family, even if you don't know the person very well. At this point, you might chat for a minute and connect about shared personal experiences. Depending on what the customer brings up when you ask about family, you might chitchat about vacation, or kids' school, or parents' health, or sports. Go with them toward whatever they bring up, and share your experiences with them.

Try to say, "I was thinking about you," or, "I thought of you because . . ."

It's really hard to be mad at you if you ask about my family and tell me you were thinking about me.

This is not something customers hear much at all.

Part Two: The Shift to the Business

After a minute or two in the opening phase, we move to the business.

There are two main questions to ask here:

- **The Did You Know (DYK) questions**, where you suggest products or services to your customers:

  - Did you know we can also help you with product x or y?

  - Do you need any product z?

  - Are you aware that we offer services a and b?

- **And the Reverse Did You Know (rDYK) questions**, where you ask the customer what additional products or services they need, above and beyond what they buy from you now:

  - What other products do you need that I can help with?

  - What other services do you buy from other providers that I can help you with?

  - What else do you need quoted?

In the DYK, you suggest products or services to your customer.

In the rDYK, the customer suggests them to you.

A few important caveats about these questions:

- They are designed to be asked in conversation, either face-to-face or, ideally, on the phone. This is because you can ask a lot of these questions to a lot of different customers and take notes on their answers.

- This means that, like most things, they are *not* particularly effective when sent by email, because emails often do not get read.

- They *can*, however, be effectively used with customers who call *you*. This is covered in my previous two books, *5-Minute Selling* and *Selling Boldly*.

- These questions should be stacked, one after the other: You can ask multiple DYKs and rDYKs to the same customers in succession. You can do them one after the other or alternate. I provide examples of both options in the scripts throughout the chapters in Part 4.

- These questions are most effective when followed with a pivot to the sale, where you help the customer lock in the order. If you ask DYKs and rDYKs without asking for the business, you will get many comments like "Oh, that's interesting," but not nearly as much business. Asking for the business is the key to getting the business. (My material is very complicated, right?)

LANGUAGE FOR SHIFTING TO THE BUSINESS

"Listen Tom, I was wondering, what projects do you have coming up that I might be able to help you with?"

or . . .

"What are you working on these days that I can help with?"

or . . .

"What do you need quoted? I'd love the opportunity to help."

or . . .

"Are your other suppliers giving you trouble with anything? Because you could give me a shot at it, and I'd love a chance to help you."

The Reverse Did You Know Is A Miracle Sales Question

The reverse did you (rDYK) questions above ask the customer to tell you about specific products and services that they need.

The rDYK is a miracle question.

You are asking the customer what they need, *and they tell you.*

They will never say to you, "No, I'd rather you not make my life easier today."

My clients have asked hundreds of thousands of these questions. They record their questions and the customers' answers. Not once did a customer say, "I don't want to be helped today."

Which is why every example question I detailed includes some version of "I'd like to help you."

The more you tell your customers and prospects that you'd like to help them, the more likely they are to work with you.

Why?

Because nobody tells them that.

They simply do not hear it from anybody else.

Just as they do not get proactive calls from suppliers when nothing is wrong.

But they will get them from you.

And they will hear that you want to help them.

When they do, they will think, "That's interesting. They want to help me. Let's see if they can."

And then, many times, they will list one or several products, projects, or services that you can help them with.

Once, a client salesperson asked his customers, "What's on your wish list that I can help with?"

He said the customer listed 24 different products.

After about five, the salesperson asked if she could please email the complete list to him.

She did.

In the first month, he sold her 18 of those products – and most of them are needed repeatedly throughout the year.

Pretty good ROI on a quick question, right?

Part Three: Pivot to the Sale or the Next Commitment

This is the third and final part of your call, where you easily figure out what happens next.

If it's remotely possible – if there's even a distant chance – ask for the business.

LANGUAGE FOR PIVOTING TO THE SALE

Ask for the business:

"Would you like me to write it up?"

"When can I expect the purchase order?"

"I can get you the proposal by end of day. When can you sign and return it?"

"How many do you want?"

"I have inventory now. Do you want me to put your name on it?"

"How would you like to pay?"

"When would you like me to start?

"I can swing by on Tuesday to pick up the contract." (Here, you are telling the customer, not asking. That's perfectly okay.)

One person recently asked, "Do you have a pen there on your desk so you can sign the agreement now?"

The question doesn't matter.

You know, many times, a customer is ready to buy, but the salesperson doesn't ask, so they don't get the business.

Sometimes I'm ready to say yes, but nobody asks for my business, so I keep the yes to myself.

Ask in a way that's comfortable and natural to you.

But ask – even if there's a tiny, single-digit-percent chance of the customer being ready to buy.

If it's not time for that yet, ask a question that cements the next interaction.

Lock in what to do next, so that you know.

If it sounds oddly simple, that's because it is.

If you don't know what to do next, and when, how can you progress the sale?

You can't.

Without a next action scheduled, you're in no-man's land.

You're not sure what the next step is, or when.

So figure it out before you hang up.

LANGUAGE FOR PIVOTING TO THE NEXT COMMITMENT

"When should we speak next?"

"What do you want me to do next?"

"When would you like me to follow up about this?"

"I can drop by Tuesday or Thursday. What's better for you?"

"I have next Wednesday at 2 PM free. Would it work for you if I called you then?"

"I'll be in your area next week. Why I don't stop by?"

"I'll put it on my calendar to check in with you midweek, okay?"

Again, the question doesn't matter.

Ask in a way that's comfortable to you.

But always, always gain commitment for the next thing.

Your customers also want to know what's next.

They don't want to spend time on the phone with you and not know what is happening next.

You should never end a call without agreeing on the next interaction.

A call is incomplete without that.

Without a next action scheduled, your selling process comes to a sudden stop at a brick wall.

Conversely, with a next action set, there's no wall.

Rather, there is a direct, smooth path to your next sale.

Most People Are Challenged by the Third Part

Most salespeople do fine with the opening and the questions that uncover what the customer or prospect needs.

But we have a hard time with the third part – the pivot to the sale or commitment.

In my work with clients, I've found that the reason for this discomfort is what we covered in depth already in this book: fear of rejection.

Asking for the next step exposes us to being told no, so we avoid it.

Of course, if we don't ask, we don't have much of a chance to get a yes, do we? *So we must risk the no to get a yes.*

I'd rather know than wonder, wouldn't you?

I'd rather get a no now than wonder for a month and get it then.

Or not get my no, and incorrectly assume the opportunity is still alive.

Let's know, so we can move on.

Either let me help you, or let me move on for a little while until I try again with you!

CHAPTER 21

SILENCE WILL MAKE YOU RICH

T his chapter is about an incredibly helpful selling technique that is wildly underused.

It is, in fact, nearly non-existent in the profession.

It causes all kinds of discomfort.

The technique is *silence.*

Yes, think of silence as a technique you should practice in every conversation you have with a customer or prospect.

Ask one of the questions in the last chapter, and then do not speak until the customer answers.

Count silently in your mind if you have to.

Sing a song if you'd like. (Not out loud.)

Do what you have to do to not talk before the customer does.

Do not nervous-chatter your way out of a sale.

"What are you working on these days that I can help you with?"

One thousand one . . . one thousand two . . . one thousand three . . .
Keep counting as long as you have to.

If the customer gives you one answer, *don't spring into action yet.*

Say, "Interesting . . ." Then, more silence.

You might say, "What else?"

Encourage the customer to share with you what else you can help with.

But no nervous chatter.

Promise me you won't talk your way out of business.

"When can I expect the P.O.?"

Jingle bells, jingle bells, jingle all the way . . .

If the customer says, "Oh, I don't know," they're still thinking. Stay out of the way!

Let them figure it out.

Don't interrupt!

IT'S OUR DISCOMFORT, NOT THE CUSTOMER'S

The customer is not quiet because they are uncomfortable, or angry with you.

Rather, they're quiet because they're *thinking*.

They hadn't thought about your question until you asked it.

You have been thinking about asking it for days or weeks, planning just the right way to ask.

But at the moment you ask, it's the first time your customer has had a chance to consider the question.

Give them a moment.

When we jump into that silence, it is because of *our* discomfort.

The sooner we realize that, the sooner it becomes easier to behave in our own best interests and help the customer do business with us.

Because this is what they want.

THE CUSTOMER SHOULD TALK AT LEAST 75% OF THE TIME

A productive ratio in a proactive call is 75–25. Let the customer talk for 75% of the conversation while you practice your silence, take notes, and ask probing follow-up questions.

This is a good ratio because it lets the customer share his or her problems with you.

It lets you learn about what they need.

It lets you uncover how you can help them.

Which is the point of our work, right?

This approach applies to face-to-face conversations as well.

What can we learn when we do all the talking?

You already know what *you* know.

And unless they specifically ask, the customer doesn't need to know what *you* know.

They simply need to know how you can help them.

And you cannot find this out unless you let the customer speak for most of the conversation.

Aim for a 75-25 ratio, and you will be in the sweet spot for successful selling.

PICK UP THE PHONE SUCCESS STORY

"There's a reason we have two ears and one mouth. I can't believe how much other salespeople talk. My entire purpose is to help the customer keep talking. That's how I learn, right? I can't learn anything if I am doing all the talking. I've made a lot of money shutting up. It's interesting to think about how uncommon that is out there. Most customers are used to just being talked at."

—Marcus Y.; independent sales rep, industrial products

CHAPTER

22

Why It's Critical to Log Your Calls

When you log your proactive calls, their outcomes, and your next steps, you create an invaluable sales resource for yourself.

Here is what to track:

Calls made
Voice messages left
New opportunities opened
Opportunities progressed
New business closed

And, of course, mark the next interaction or the next commitment you have scheduled with your customer or prospect at the end of the call.

This way, you will know what to do next.

In fact, you'll have a powerful list of next actions and an incredible reference of customers and prospects who can buy – or buy more – from you.

The Proactive Call Tracker

Week Of (Date):

Enter calls made, voicemails left, opportunities opened, opportunities progressed, and new business closed.

Date	Customer Name & Company	Products or Services Discussed & Outcomes	$ Value	Follow-Up Date & Action

Here are all of the benefits of logging your communications with customers or prospects:

More than anything else, you create an invaluable list of opportunities to follow up on. You will be able to easily see who you talked with, which products and services were discussed, and when the next communication needs to happen. It's a goldmine of opportunities, created by you. **The Proactive Call Tracker will remind you of all the opportunities before you.** You're so busy that in a typical day, the phone rarely stops ringing. If you don't log your calls, you won't remember the opportunities you uncovered, or when to follow up on them.

When you don't know who to call, you can make your follow-up calls directly from the log. Every person listed there was called before and can be called again.

This list will be proof of your success. You did the things on this list. You created them with your effort, determination, and perseverance. They did not exist, and then you made your call(s), and now they do. You did that.

This list will help you deal with the fear of picking up the phone. Fear is persistent: just because you've made some successful proactive calls that generated new opportunities and sales doesn't mean your fear will totally go away. You'll still have to overcome it the next time you go to make proactive calls. So when it's time to pick up the phone for the first time on a new day and you find yourself in need of some enthusiasm, positivity, or proof of your success to help you overcome your fear of rejection, look at your Proactive Call Tracker and let it remind you how good you are.

All those people on the list know how good you are.

If you work with other salespeople on a team, you can share your Proactive Call Trackers with each other. This way, everyone will know who was contacted, what was said, what worked and did not work, and what the outcomes were. You might even hold a regularly scheduled discussion of your proactive calling successes, as my clients do.

Your sales manager and executive leadership can quickly get a sense of the opportunities uncovered, progressed, or closed. This creates a communications loop of positive sales achievements and allows them to offer feedback, suggestions, and recognition. Believe it or not, management wants to have positive conversations with colleagues, but by the time most things reach their desk, they are challenges or problems. Your Proactive Call Tracker will bring them positive results on a regular basis.

Use the Proactive Call Tracker to track your opportunities, log your follow-ups, and remind you of your incredible effectiveness.

It will quickly help you grow your sales.

PICK UP THE PHONE SUCCESS STORY

"I know some people feel like it's a chore to log our calls, but I feel like I'm a better salesperson when I log them. It helps me know everything I did and everything I need to follow up on. Sometimes it's a lifesaver because I would not have remembered to follow up if it wasn't written down in front of me in my call tracker. I even take the log with me into the car when I go visit customers and make a bunch of follow-up calls right from the logs while I drive. I have absolutely closed sales because of the Proactive Call Tracker that I would not have otherwise gotten."

—George C.; client executive, engineering firm

PART FOUR

WHO SHOULD YOU CALL? MOSTLY, CALL PEOPLE YOU KNOW

23

CHAPTER

You Know Hundreds of People Who Can Buy from You – Call Them!

U nless you're just start-
ing out in sales, you know hundreds of customers and prospects.

But most salespeople assume that calling automatically
means cold calling.

Early in my client work, I would suggest making proactive
calls, and nearly every time, salespeople reacted with, "I *hate*
cold calls."

We are so uncomfortable with making phone calls that we
instantly jump to the worst possible kind of call – one where
we don't know the person we are calling, and they hate us!

Let me clarify preemptively: when I say *make proactive calls*,
I mean *call people you know when nothing is wrong*.

I acknowledge that a minority of salespeople must make
cold calls. That's that job, and that's how they make a living.

I also accept that many salespeople feel they've arrived
at a point where they've called the customers and prospects
they know, and now they must move on to calling people they
do not know.

I would like to suggest to this latter group of salespeople
that you *know* a whole lot of customers and prospects who
would like to hear from you. And they would like to buy from
you and work with you.

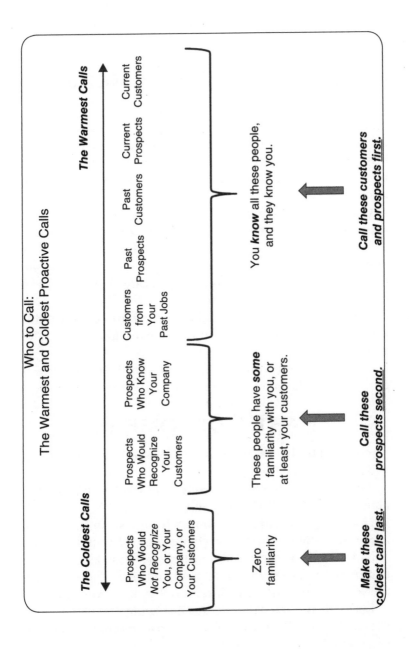

Who to Call:
The Warmest and Coldest Proactive Calls

The Warmest Calls

The Coldest Calls

| Prospects Who Would Not Recognize You, or Your Company, or Your Customers | Prospects Who Would Recognize Your Customers | Prospects Who Know Your Company | Customers from Your Past Jobs | Past Prospects | Past Customers | Current Prospects | Current Customers |

Zero familiarity

These people have **some** familiarity with you, or at least, your customers.

You **know** all these people, and they know you.

Make these coldest calls last.

Call these prospects second.

Call these customers and prospects first.

In this part of the book, I lay out all the different categories and groups of customers and prospects who you know and can call.

CURRENT CUSTOMERS

You are working with them now. They are buying from you – and they can buy more. Almost all of us have customers who are buying things from the competition that they could be buying from us. Let's call them, check on them, and ask what else they need, or offer additional products or services we know they could use.

Calling current customers to help them more and expand your business with them is the low-hanging fruit in sales. They're with you already. They've been with you for years. They know how good you are. They value you. Now you're showing up, demonstrating to them that you care about them, and offering to help them some more.

For most salespeople, making proactive calls to this group of customers will create your biggest and fastest sales growth.

I will take you through calling different kinds of current customers in the coming chapters in this part of the book.

PAST CUSTOMERS

These are people who used to buy from you but stopped.

They've moved on.

They probably moved on quietly, and you haven't thought about many of them in some time.

Don't forget your past customers from your previous jobs, and past customers who have changed jobs themselves.

Now that these past customers have been working with the competition, they know what they are missing. These are people you used to work with closely, so they know your value.

Let's call and offer them that value again.

Details on proactive calls to past customers are in Chapter 30.

CURRENT PROSPECTS

This is a group of people you are having active buying conversations with, but they have not bought from you yet.

Some salespeople avoid calling this group because they feel it's best not to bother them.

They don't want to risk rejection.

I'm a strong proponent of calling these current prospects, checking in with them, telling them you are thinking about them, and asking where they are in their decision because you'd like to help them.

PAST PROSPECTS

These are the hardest people to remember and list on the planner.

You talked about business, you discussed a purchase, but it did not happen.

They talked to you, they know your name and your company name, and they got part way down the path of buying from you.

Let's call these people.

Tell them we remember them.

And ask how we can help them.

More on this group in Chapter 32.

THESE CALLS ARE LIGHTNING FAST

If you're thinking about how busy you are and wondering how in the world you will find time to make these calls, I want to remind you that most proactive calls will result in you leaving a voice message. This means they will take less than one minute.

On the other hand, if the customer picks up and you follow the quick three-part call scripts laid out in Chapter 20 and discussed in detail in the upcoming chapters, your conversations will last an average of five minutes. *Maybe* 10 minutes, at the most.

These 5- to 10-minute calls will almost always result in new opportunities opened, progressed, or closed.

That's a pretty good use of your time!

THE UPCOMING CHAPTERS

The following chapters in this part of the book list nine groups of customers and prospects who you know and who will recognize your name or your company name.

Many of these customers can buy more from you.

Some of them already have a quote from you, so your call will remind them to pull the trigger.

Some of them email you daily but almost never hear your voice.

And some are simply on auto-pilot – house accounts by default.

Is there some overlap in the customers in the coming pages? Sure, but that's on purpose. My goal is to help you *think of who to call,* and if some of your customers fall into multiple categories, so be it. Write them down, make a plan, and then pick up the phone.

HOW TO PLAN WHO TO CALL

Keep a running list of your target customers and prospects to communicate with on the Target 60 Sales Success Planner. Fill this out, or refresh it, at the start of every month.

Start on the right, and work toward the left. First, identify 30 current customers and what else they can buy. Then list 20 prospects you've already spoken with. And then write out 10 prospects you have not talked to yet but want to. This will keep an updated list of your top-priority customers and prospects in front of you, which will make it easy to pick up the phone – *because you will know who to call.*

The names of these people are sometimes difficult to think of, because they usually don't call us, and we are busy talking to others, who *do* call.

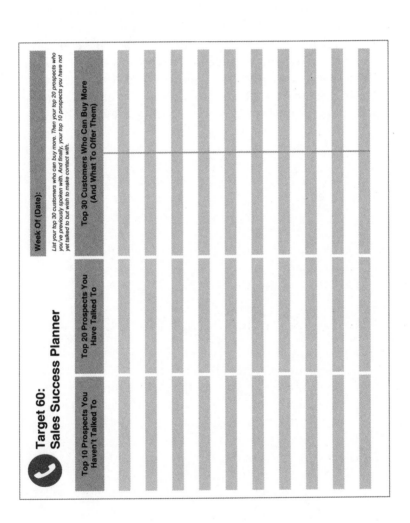

Target 60:
Sales Success Planner

Week Of (Date):

List your top 30 customers who can buy more. Then your top 20 prospects who you've previously spoken with. And finally, your top 10 prospects you have not yet talked to but wish to make contact with.

Top 10 Prospects You Haven't Talked To	Top 20 Prospects You Have Talked To	Top 30 Customers Who Can Buy More (And What To Offer Them)

So, let's spend a few minutes per week planning who to call, and we will never wonder who needs to hear from us. (Let the competition not know who to call!)

You can use your Target 60 planner as a reference when you fill out your weekly Simple Proactive Call Planner in 5 to 10 minutes on Sunday or Monday morning. With this planner, you'll always know who to call when the time comes.

There is so much value – to the customer *and* the salesperson – in calling these good people that I can't think of a single activity of greater impact on sales growth. Time to pick up the phone and reap the exciting sales benefits!

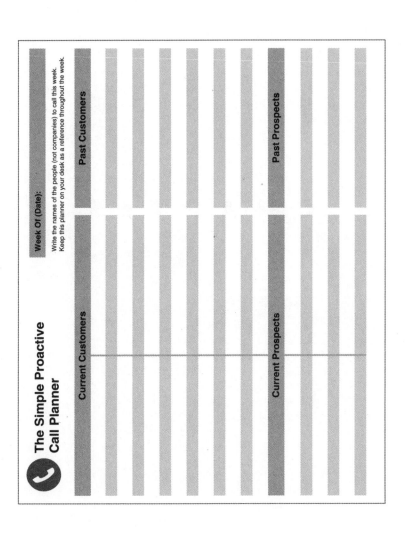

The Simple Proactive Call Planner

Week Of (Date):

Write the names of the people (not companies) to call this week.
Keep this planner on your desk as a reference throughout the week.

Current Customers

Past Customers

Current Prospects

Past Prospects

CHAPTER 24

CALL CUSTOMERS WHO CAN BUY MORE FROM YOU

H ere is a truth about customers: Our customers niche us.

They buy certain things from us and certain things from others.

Even though we can sell them these other products or services they buy from others, they go elsewhere for them.

Why?

Two big reasons: First, because we salespeople also niche our customers.

They buy what they buy, and if they want something else, they'll ask me for it.

Of course, it doesn't work this way – they *can't* ask you for it, because they simply don't know they can buy it from you.

They don't think about you for these other products.

Which brings me to the second reason that your customers go elsewhere: because they almost never hear from salespeople, including you, proactively, when nothing is wrong.

Almost nobody calls customers to ask them what projects or jobs they have coming up that you can help them with.

Nobody calls customers to ask them what else they buy elsewhere.

Almost all customers buy on autopilot, with little proactive involvement from salespeople.

The proactive calls laid out in this chapter will solve this issue.

And the solution can be incredibly valuable for you.

In fact, the solution can make you rich.

ABOUT THIS GROUP OF CUSTOMERS

These are your large, medium, and small customers.

Many of them have been with you for years.

They are happy, generally. Your service their account very well. You deliver accurately and on time. You're available to them when they call. Your customer service is world-class.

Because of this, these customers rarely call you.

They buy what they buy, and you're happy to accept the orders and take care of them.

WHY CALL THEM?

- Because there's so much more they can buy from you.
- Because there's so much more you can help them with.
- Because you should actively try to rescue them from the competition. Why should they have to suffer through the competition when they can buy from you?
- Because it will be easier for your customers to buy what they need from one excellent supplier – you – than from three or four suppliers.
- It will save them time.
- It will make their lives easier.

Call them to make their lives easier.

Call them to help them more.

It's what they want.

Your Script: What to Say to Customers Who Can Buy More

The Opening

Hi Joe, it's Alex Goldfayn. I was thinking about you and wanted to pick up the phone. How are you? How's your family? Are the kids doing well?

The Shift to Business

Listen, I wanted to thank you for your recent order, and I was wondering, what other products do you buy elsewhere that I can help you with? Because I'd like to help you more.

and/or . . .

What projects do you have coming up? I'd love to help you with those.

and/or . . .

What else do you need quoted?

and/or . . .

I wanted to let you know that I noticed prices are going up on some of these materials next month. Would you like to add some at current pricing?

A few notes:

1. Feel free to combine these. More than one is perfectly fine. Stack them.

2. I've given you four reverse did you know (rDYK) questions here (as detailed in Chapter 20), but there's no reason you can't come up with your own that work

well for you. You probably know exactly what questions you might ask that have worked well for you previously.

3. Remember to ask the questions and then be silent. Let your customer think. Don't chatter your way out of additional products or services.

Now, Pivot to the Sale

I wrote everything down, Tom, and I'll get you a quote shortly. When can I expect a P.O. on this?

or . . .

When would you like these delivered?

or . . .

I can have this out to you next week.

A couple of notes:

1. In the final example, note that the pivot to the sale is a statement, not a question. You can ask for the business with a statement like this. It's almost *assuming* the close, isn't it?

2. Once again, silence is critically important. Ask, and then wait for an answer. They're not silent because they're uncomfortable. They're silent because they're thinking. Let them.

Call your good customers who can buy more.

Ask them what else they need, or what they buy elsewhere, or what project they have coming up (the rDYK).

Or *tell* them what else you can sell or do for them (the DYK).

And watch your new sales pile up.

This is what you will do – if you pick up the phone and sell.

PICK UP THE PHONE SUCCESS STORY

"My calls almost always go to customers who order from us steady. I just ask them what else they need this week or what else they want me to throw on the truck for them. And they give me additional products every . . . single . . . time. All I gotta do is ask. I ask, and they order! [Laughing.]"

—Bradley Z.; outside sales, manufacturer

CHAPTER

25

CALL CUSTOMERS WHO JUST RECEIVED PRODUCTS OR SERVICES

Can you remember the last time you bought something and the salesperson followed up to ask you if you were pleased with what you bought?

Car salespeople used to do this, but I have not received a post-purchase call from a car dealer in probably a decade.

What about other purchases, personal or work-related? Have you heard from the salespeople?

Nobody really does this any more.

Which is why we should.

ABOUT THIS GROUP
OF CUSTOMERS

These are customers who recently received a product or service from you.

They can be big, medium, or small customers.

They placed an order, you sent it or did the work, and now you're calling them to follow up.

WHY CALL THEM?

- To check on your customer.

- To communicate that you care about them and want to make sure they're good.

- To make sure your products arrived on time and accurately.

- To separate yourself from the competition, because they are not doing this.

- To be dependable: to show your customer that you not only do what you say you will do (which is, somewhat surprisingly, very rare in business) but also call them to make sure everything went well.

- To proactively fix any problems with this order that may have come up.

- To make sure your customer doesn't have other issues with other products and services beyond the order you are calling to check on.

- This is a customer service call, ultimately.

- And, most importantly, to see about what else your customer needs.

YOUR SCRIPT: WHAT TO SAY TO CUSTOMERS WHO JUST RECEIVED PRODUCTS OR SERVICE FROM YOU

The Opening

Hi Jennifer, it's Louis. How are you doing? How's your family? Are the kids ready for a new school year?

The Shift to Business

I was thinking about you and wanted to check in on your most recent order. Did everything arrive okay?

All good with that? Do you need anything else on that order?

or, if you provide a service . . .

I was thinking about you because I wanted to make sure everything went well with our recent work. All good? Is there anything else I can help you with on that project?

Then go to your rDYK question:

Great to hear! I was wondering, what other projects do you have coming up that I can help you with? I'd love to help.

or . . .

Great! What else do you need quoted?

or . . .

I'm happy to hear that. What other products (or services) do you need that I can help with?

Note: You are making sure the products arrived successfully or the services were delivered to the customer's satisfaction. This is not a sales call but a customer service communication. The customer will be stunned with gratitude that somebody cares enough to pick up the phone and ask. Easy. No pressure!

Now, Pivot to the Sale

Excellent! Should I write that up for you?

or . . .

Got it. Would you like me to ship that out this week or next week?

or . . .

Okay, I'm on it. When would like us to do this?

You know what's great about this phone call?
Nobody else is doing it.

Your customer has not heard from anyone like this, maybe ever!

Try connecting with each of your customers on a post-delivery call like this three or four times a year at a minimum.

You will be rewarded with their loyalty.

And they will thank you with additional business.

PICK UP THE PHONE SUCCESS STORY

"The other day, I called a customer who we did a service call for. I asked her if everything is working well now and if she needs anything else with that issue with her furnace. She said everything is great and told me how much she appreciates that I checked in with her. I asked her if she needed anything else with her other furnaces or air conditioners in the buildings, and I told her we have a preventative maintenance program as well, so we can address issues before they cause her problems. She told me about some other problems that are worrying her, and we have a call booked to discuss our annual maintenance. I would not have booked this appointment without checking in with her."

—Sandra E.; client relations, HVAC contractor

CHAPTER

26

CALL CUSTOMERS WHO HAVEN'T MADE THEIR REGULAR PURCHASE IN A WHILE

We all have customers who used to buy but stopped.

If you had a customer who used a product or service regularly but stopped, this person hasn't stopped buying this product or service.

They've simply stopped buying it from you.

So this proactive call is to reconnect with them.

To tell them you'd like to help them again.

To remind them that they used to buy this from you, and you'd like to take care of them again.

ABOUT THIS GROUP OF CUSTOMERS

These customers used to buy a variety of products or services from you and do business with you regularly.

But suddenly their purchases of one or more products stopped.

Maybe you noticed – but you probably didn't, because you're busy.

They didn't tell you they were moving their business for this product or products to another supplier.

Also, they didn't call you, because they may not have even known they were leaving you yet.

Most likely, what happened was that a competitor reached out to them and offered them the same or a similar product or service at a lower price.

So the customer "gave it a try."

They gave the other guys a chance on these items or services.

And they've been buying from the competition ever since.

They may still buy some products or services from you, but they've moved some of their business away.

How to Identify These Customers

Go to your order history or your invoice history.

Open your customer's record in your ERP system or even in QuickBooks.

If none of those are options, go to your email history or your contact list.

Look for people who used to buy regularly – weekly, monthly, quarterly – any rhythmic buying.

These are your customers for these calls.

Another Possibility That Happens Frequently

A significant number of these order history calls turn into business for my clients not because the customer moved their business elsewhere, but simply because *they forgot to reorder!*

When my clients ask the customer if they need more of these items or services, the answer is frequently something like, "Oh, yes! Thank you for reminding me!"

WHY CALL THEM?

- Because they are still likely buying the product(s) that they used to get regularly from you.

- Because if they needed it for months or years, they probably didn't suddenly stop needing it.

- And they're still probably a customer on other items.

- So let's go back and see about helping them again with the products they moved away.

- To tell them you'd like to help with those products again. They'll be pleased to hear from you.

Even if you don't get the business back immediately, you will plant a seed with the customer, and before long, they may be calling you to reorder.

YOUR SCRIPT: WHAT TO SAY TO CUSTOMERS WHO USED TO BUY SOMETHING REGULARLY BUT STOPPED

The Opening

Hello Mark, it's Sandra Jones. How are you? Been a long time since we've talked! I was thinking about you, so I wanted to pick up the phone and connect. How are you? How is your family? The last time we talked, you were heading for a trip to Cancun, I think – any good vacations lately?

The Shift to Business

Listen, I remember you used to buy product x or service y from us on a regular basis, but I haven't seen any orders come through for several months. Do you still have a need for that?

If yes, and if they moved their business somewhere else:

Well, I'd love to earn your business for that again. Plus I miss you, and I'd love to help you again.

or . . .

> *I see. What would it take to earn your business again? Because it's important to me to help you again.*

And the rDYK:

> *What other products are you buying from those guys that I can help you with?*

or . . .

> *What other products do you need that I can help you with?*

or . . .

> *What else do you have coming up that I can assist on?*

Now, Pivot to the Sale

> *I have one in stock. When would you like it?*

or . . .

> *I can put them on a truck for delivery Thursday. Would that work?*

or, if a service . . .

> *I can get out there to meet with you next week, if that works for you.*

These customers need you.

This proactive call is a perfect way to show them that you're here for them.

You miss them.

And you want to help them again.

Nobody hears this.

And when they hear from you this way, it will be nearly impossible for your customer to say no.

PICK UP THE PHONE
SUCCESS STORY

"After our training, I went through my customer list and called a customer who regularly bought drains from us for years but hadn't in a few months. We talked about life and family for a few minutes, and then I asked him if he needed any more drains. He told me he was nearly out of them and was meaning to call me to order more and hadn't been able to get around to it. So he just got busy, and I reminded him. He placed the order on that call."

—Colette F.; customer service, distributor

CHAPTER 27

CALL CUSTOMERS WHO EMAIL YOU ORDERS AND INQUIRIES

E very day, you get emails.
Endless emails, right?

Many are junk, but the ones that aren't junk include

- Incoming orders

- Service issues you need to resolve

- Inquiries about your products and services

Most of these emails require a response from you, and a rather time-sensitive one. You have to take action on almost all of them.

What if, once or twice a day, you picked up the phone and called somebody who emailed you?

Reply with a phone call to one or two of these emails that contain orders and questions and inquiries about your products or services.

It's a brilliant and simple technique that has generated millions of dollars in sales for my clients.

About This Group of Customers

These are good customers who are mostly on auto-pilot.

They buy a few of your products, usually by email or through some other electronic ordering pathway.

They don't call you much, if ever, and you don't call them, because you're busy dealing with the customers who call with problems and urgencies all day.

So they buy without much interaction.

They buy on their own.

And yet these customers deliver sales that you count on to hit your numbers every year.

Why Call Them?

- Because they deserve your attention.
- They're good to you. They're dependable.
- They would appreciate hearing from you, and *they would appreciate knowing what else they can buy from you.*
- Which is the second major reason to call this group proactively: they are buying from you only a small fraction of everything they would benefit from.

So let's pick up the phone, provide a very pleasant surprise, connect with a good customer, pour cement on our relationship with them (bringing them even closer to you), and explore the other products and services we can provide.

Your Script: What to Say to Customers Who Email Orders and Inquiries

The Opening

Hi George, it's Kate. How are you? I hope your family is well and that your grandkids are doing great. I got your email, and it made me think of you, so I wanted to pick up the phone and say hello.

The Shift to Business

"Of course, I will get right on processing that order you emailed in, but I wanted to ask a couple of questions as well."

Two or three DYKs:

Did you know we also provide products (or services) x, y, and z?

Now an rDYK:

What other products (or services) did you need with that?

And another rDYK – no need to stop at one:

What other projects or initiatives do you have coming up that I can help you with?

Why not one more?

Interesting, I got it. Need anything else quoted while we're talking? Why should you have to remember it and think about it again later if we're on the phone now? I'd love to help while we're talking.

The Pivot to the Sale

Okay, I got all of it. Do you want me to make it all one order, or should I write it up separately?

or . . .

When would you like all this delivered?

or . . .

I can have all this to you on Wednesday.

As always, make your pivot to the sale, and then be silent.

Let the customer consider your question or suggestion to buy, and let them answer.

Imagine if you made one or two of these kinds of proactive calls a day.

That would be 5 to 10 a week.

On top of your other proactive work.

How could your business *not* grow dramatically?

That's the thing:

If you picked up the phone to make these calls, your sales would have *no choice* but to grow.

Plus, as an added bonus, you'd have pleasant, warm conversations with customers who were happy to hear from you.

They'd feel good, you'd feel good, your company would grow, and you'd take home more money to your family.

There is *only* upside here, and literally no downside.

PICK UP THE PHONE SUCCESS STORY

"I'm in inside sales, and my customers send in email orders constantly. I made a proactive call to a good customer this morning, and we realized we hadn't talked on the phone in over a year! I asked what else I can help him with, and he told me about a project they have coming up that I wouldn't have known about otherwise. It turned into a $12,000 order on the spot, and a bunch of the items were the first time he has ever bought those from us. He said he didn't know he could buy those items from us."

—Joseph E.; outside sales, manufacturer

CHAPTER

28

CALL CUSTOMERS WHO HAVE A QUOTE OR PROPOSAL

Salespeople regularly send quotes and proposals to customers.

Some customers say yes quickly.

Others say yes down the road.

But very few customers say no.

People don't like to say no.

So in sales, it tends to be either yes or nothing.

Yes or silence.

This call is about following up and checking on their intentions for the quote or proposals you sent.

ABOUT THIS GROUP OF CUSTOMERS

These are customers you have built relationships with.

You've serviced their accounts for years.

You've been available.

You've been accurate, timely, and responsive in your dealings with these customers.

Now they've asked you for a quote.

You stop what you're doing and write the quote or proposal.

And then, many times, you wait.

There is no response from the customer.

Meanwhile, we're hesitant and tentative to follow up because we don't want to get rejected.

If we call to ask about the quote, they might say no!

They might also say yes, but that's beside the point in our fear-based avoidance.

The fear is much stronger than the possibility of getting a yes.

We'd rather not ask for a yes than risk getting a no!

Plus, there's this nonsense (which makes perfect sense when wrapped up in our fear): if I'm not hearing anything, that means I'm still alive. The deal can still happen.

We use this twisted logic to justify our reticence for picking up the phone.

The Customer Is Rarely Quiet Because They Don't Want to Buy

My client salespeople have implemented and tracked and recorded the results of hundreds of thousands of quote follow-ups.

When detailing their experiences, they find the most frequent reasons customers do not respond to quotes are that:

They forget.

Or they get busy.

Remember, they *asked* you for this quote. You are not sending them a quote against their will. They wanted it.

Which is why it makes sense that when my clients call these customers who have their quote or proposal, the customers are extremely appreciative.

They thank my clients.

And then they buy.

WHY CALL THEM?

Call these customers because you have done 99% of the work on this order, up to and including sending the quote.

The last 1% is following up on the quote and asking for the business.

That's what this call is.

The last 1%.

The customer deserves the opportunity to buy this from you. *They deserve your help within the buying process.*

This call is you helping the customer buy from you.

YOUR SCRIPT: WHAT TO SAY TO CUSTOMERS WHO HAVE A QUOTE OR PROPOSAL

The Opening

Hi Joe, it's Andy from XYZ Company. How are you? How's your family? Everybody doing well? Hope you're handling all this weather we've had!

The Shift to Business

I was thinking about you because I'm wondering where you're at on that quote we talked about. I'd love to help you with that.

or . . .

I had sent you over that proposal after our last conversation – did you get it? Sometimes these things can get picked off by spam filters. I'd love to help you with that if you still need the products (or services).

or . . .

Listen, I wanted to let you know that the quote (or proposal) is expiring in about 48 hours, and I wanted to check in with you to make sure you don't lose the pricing we worked out.

Note that all three of these follow-ups are great efforts that have closed hundreds of millions of dollars in business for my clients.

They all work well, but the expiration follow-up is incredibly effective. (See my client's story at the end of this chapter.)

Now, ask your rDYK:

What else do you need that we can take care of for you now?

or . . .

What other projects do you have coming up that I can write up for you here while we're talking?

Now, Pivot to the Sale

So when can I expect your P.O.?

or . . .

So you'll send me the P.O. by end of tomorrow, before the expiration?

You will be amazed how many quotes you close following this model.

One of my clients, a large distributor, improved their close rate from 20% to 82% by following up systematically on quotes.

Another went from an 18% close rate to 61%.

Always remember that your customers *want you* to follow up.

They appreciate it.

You're not bothering them.

By reminding them, you are helping them.

And you are saving them time.

Do you think they want to go through the quote or proposal creation process again?

Or worse, with somebody else?

No. Of course not.

They want to buy from you.

When you call, you are simply helping them with this.

They will reward you with their purchase order.

PICK UP THE PHONE
SUCCESS STORY

"I am pleasantly surprised every time I remind a customer of a quote that's going to expire. About 75% of the time, they place the order or schedule delivery for that very same day. And they always appreciate me reminding them. How great is that?"

—Shelly F.; showroom salesperson,
home remodeling distributor

CHAPTER 29

CALL CUSTOMERS YOU HAVEN'T TALKED TO IN THREE MONTHS OR MORE

I have a question for you: Out of all of your customers – including the small and medium-sized ones – what percent would you guess you haven't talked with in three months or more?

In my experience with clients, this number is easily more than half and often approaches 80%.

That's upward of 8 out of 10 customers who simply haven't heard from their salesperson in over three months.

Amazingly, during this time, these people have still made their repeat purchases, operating on autopilot.

ABOUT THIS GROUP OF CUSTOMERS

Like nearly all of your customers who are quiet, these customers are quite happy, which is why they've been with you for years, returning without fail for the products that they've always bought from you.

Like you, they're very busy.

Like you, they're constantly servicing *their* customers.

And, just as you get calls from customers who have problems, *those* customers also call the suppliers they are having problems with, but you are not one of them.

So, they're good.

They're happy with you and your work.

Which is exactly why you must reach out.

WHY CALL THEM?

- Because in many ways, these customers are our lowest-hanging fruit for sales growth.

- They buy many other products or services that you can help them with, but you don't talk to them about that.

- Because you don't talk to them about anything, really, because you don't talk to these customers.

So, let's pick up the phone, work on our relationship with a brief conversation about family and work, and then explore what else they're buying elsewhere and what we can help them with.

YOUR SCRIPT: WHAT TO SAY TO CUSTOMERS YOU HAVEN'T TALKED TO IN THREE MONTHS OR MORE

The Opening

Hello Brittany, it's Rachel Thompson calling. How are you? I was thinking about you because I saw your recent order come in, and I wanted to let you know how much we appreciate your trust and business all these years. How are you? How's your family?

The Shift to Business

> *Brittany, I realized it has been a while since we talked, so I wanted to ask if you're using any other products (or services) that I can help you with.*

Ask the first rDYK:

> *What are you buying from other suppliers that I can help with?*

Now ask another rDYK:

> *What else can I quote for you? I'd like to help you more.*

Feel free to suggest some products with some DYKs:

> *Do you need any x or y? What about product z? Do you use any of that on your projects?*

Now, Pivot to the Sale

> *Would you like me to add these to your current order, or should we write it up separately?*

or . . .

> *Should we use the standing P.O., or would you prefer to send me a different one for this?*

Don't allow these customers to buy from you on autopilot. Don't make them go to the competition for products and services you can help them with.

They're good to you – and unlike your other customers, they require little time and attention.

Call them proactively.

Tell them you'd like to help them more.

And watch the new sales pour in.

PICK UP THE PHONE
SUCCESS STORY

"I didn't realize how many customers I have who I don't talk to until I looked at our invoices over the last few months. I think about 80% of the customers who place orders with us don't talk to us. I've made it a point to call these customers, if nothing else than because there are so many of them! I've enjoyed reconnecting with them. It's great to catch up and hear about what's happening in their lives. They're all so happy to hear from me. This has absolutely led to new business from these customers. I learned that they appreciate me, and I told them the same. It's a win-win all around."

—Tommy D.; salesperson,
water treatment product distributor

CHAPTER 30

CALL CUSTOMERS WHO USED TO BUY FROM YOU, BUT STOPPED

This chapter is about making proactive calls to your ex-customers.

These are not people who have moved a product or two away from you or shifted to a competitor on a single service that you offer.

These folks have left you for the competition.

They may not be *happy* with the competition, but they're buying from them, not from you.

These calls are about inviting them back.

ABOUT THIS GROUP OF CUSTOMERS

These customers bought from you for a long time.

Then perhaps there was a problem.

Or maybe they had a difficult experience that didn't sit well with them. Mistakes happen. You're human, and so are your colleagues, and frankly, nobody expects you to be perfect. But customers expect you to make it right, and perhaps something happened that didn't go so smoothly.

But maybe not.

Maybe the competition simply reached out and offered cheaper pricing.

You know the competition – happy to undercut, happy to trim their margin to razor-thin levels, often damaging the entire industry in the process.

So, now, these customers buy elsewhere.

They may have left months ago, or years ago.

It's never too late to call them and tell them you'd like to help them again.

How to Identify These Customers

This is a challenging group of customers to list, because sometimes *we don't even know they've gone away from us.*

So look in your CRM system, which lists your customers and prospects.

Also, go into your quote log and invoices.

And your emails.

And your phone's contact list.

Look for people who used to buy regularly but then stopped.

These are your people!

WHY CALL THEM?

These customers used to do a lot of business with you – or at least they did business with you regularly.

Then, suddenly, without you noticing, the orders stopped.

They gave someone else a chance, and sort of drifted away from you.

Now you will come back to them, let them know you are thinking about them, and ask to serve them again.

YOUR SCRIPT: WHAT TO SAY TO CUSTOMERS WHO USED TO BUY FROM YOU BUT STOPPED

The Opening

Hi Richard, it's Sam Welles calling from XYZ Manufacturing. How are you? It has been a while, hasn't it? Good to hear your voice. I thought of you because I just had a customer order some products you used to buy all the time, and it made me realize I needed to pick up the phone and call you. How's your family doing?

The Shift to Business

As with all of our scripts, be honest, straightforward, and clear that you'd like to help your customer again. Don't spend a lot of time getting into what was wrong when they left, but rather, that you'd like to help them again.

I was thinking about the business we used to do together, and I have to tell you, I'd love the opportunity to earn it back.

or . . .

We miss you around here, Richard. I'd love to help you again. How would you feel about giving us another shot?

or . . .

What would it take for us to get you back? Because that's important to me. I'd love to work with you again.

Remember, ask these rather direct (and probably somewhat uncomfortable) questions, and then quietly let the customer think and answer your question.

No rDYKs or DYKs here. You're just looking to get the first order back. Bring those questions the *next* time you talk, if the customer takes a step back to you in this conversation.

Now, Pivot to the Sale

I took a look before I called, Richard. We have some of your product in stock. Would you like me to put it on a truck for you?

or . . .

You still have credit with us – do you want me to get your order out? I'll see it through personally and will do so from now on. Are you still ordering in the same quantity?

or . . .

We can start your service next month if that aligns with your current schedule.

Go back to these folks.

They will be impressed with this effort.

It's not like others are trying to win them over like this.

Show up and be present, and let them hear that you care enough to get them back.

I'd give better than 50-50 odds that they'll reward you with some of their business again.

PICK UP THE PHONE SUCCESS STORY

"I used to really dislike making sales calls because I thought people didn't want to talk to me. What I've found since I started following your approaches is that my customers are happy to hear from me. They ask about me and how I'm doing. Before, I thought I was bothering them. Now I know they like that I call them. You know what I've found? The more customers I call, the more I talk to people, the more money I make. That seems like common sense, but I didn't believe that until I started doing it."

—Marcie J.; customer service manager, manufacturer

CHAPTER 31

CALL CUSTOMERS WHO ARE HOUSE ACCOUNTS AND RARELY HEAR FROM YOUR COMPANY

Among my manufacturer and distributor clients, about 20% of the customers have an account rep who they are regularly in touch with.

These customers have a point of contact.

They have a name, and a phone number, and an email address.

Sometimes, the salespeople even reach out to these customers. In my experience, this happens rarely, and only the biggest of these 20% hear from their salesperson with any frequency.

This leaves 80% of the remaining customers without a sales contact who oversees their account.

Officially, they may have a salesperson assigned.

But that person is very busy with incoming urgencies and problems, as well as his or her top 20% of customers. That leaves little to no time for the 80%.

As we discussed in Chapter 10, this makes most of these 80% of customers house accounts by default.

They are untethered, without a human connection to your organization.

The only connection that exists is incoming, made by them, when they place their orders electronically.

About This Group of Customers

These house-accounts-by-default are good, easy customers.

They make their orders, usually without bothering anybody.

They know what they buy from you, they know they'll get quality and timeliness, and they keep going back to the well for it. It works; why change?

These are also satisfied customers. They're pleased. That's why they keep coming back to you, even though they don't really have a contact point.

They are satisfied accounts, buying on their own, without assistance or intervention from salespeople.

Why Call Them?

We call these customers because they are the least-communicated-with customers you have.

They're also loyal.

They appreciate buying from your company – they value you.

They depend on you.

It's a recipe for huge potential sales growth because there's so much more we can help them with. There's so much more they can buy.

They don't even know what else they can buy from us because they're not connected to anybody in sales. They have nobody to tell them,

So we surprise them by calling them proactively.

And we try to help them and expand our business with them.

Your Script: What to Say to Customers Who Are House Accounts

The Opening

Hi Pete, it's Mark Hopkins from XYZ company. How are you? I know we haven't talked before, but I'm an account manager here, and I thought of you because I see your orders come across regularly. So I wanted to pick up the phone and learn a bit more about your work and understand how things are going overall with us.

The Shift to Business

Ask the first rDYK:

What other products or services do you typically buy?

and the second rDYK:

What kinds of projects do you work on?

At this point, you can go to a DYK:

That's interesting. Did you know we sell products x, y, and z for those kinds of projects?

Back to an rDYK:

What do you buy from others that we can help you with?

As always, follow each question with silence to let your customer think about their answer.

Now, Pivot to the Sale

Okay, great, let me write all this up for you. I'm honored by the opportunity to help you. When do you think you can get us the P.O.?

or . . .

>*I can have all this put together for you by early in the week. Should we send it out for delivery right away, or do you want us to hold it for a particular date?*

or . . .

>*We can start service next week, if that's good for you.*

Go to these customers who have no contact at your company. They don't have a person they can rely on.

So you be their person.

Help them.

And they'll help you with more business.

PICK UP THE PHONE SUCCESS STORY

"There are people on my team who refuse to make phone calls to clients. They feel that it's not their job. They didn't become engineers to sell, they say. 'I'm not a salesperson, and I'm too busy for this anyway.' Well, how do you know what your clients need if you're not talking to them? What if they need something else, and you can help, and you don't know it because you're not calling them? I started making just one unscheduled call every morning to people at my client companies, and it has really brought us closer. We know about each other's kids and personal lives. Guess who these clients go to when they need something: the project manager they know, who makes an effort, or the ones who never call?"

—Gary P.; project manager, engineering company

CHAPTER

32

CALL PROSPECTS YOU'VE TALKED TO BUT WHO NEVER BOUGHT FROM YOU

F inally, after eight chapters about different customers you can call to significantly grow your sales with them, we've arrived at prospects.

These prospects are people you know. You've talked before.

In fact, you've discussed doing business previously, but it didn't come together.

Perhaps they almost bought.

Perhaps you met in person and discussed the framework of the products and services you might provide.

In my sales growth consulting practice, I have a lot of people like this, who considered working with me but didn't pull the trigger.

And every year, some prospects from this group become clients.

Why?

Because I reach out to them regularly.

They hear from me.

I stay in touch.

I keep trying to help.

Because that's my job.
And your job.
That's the work.

ABOUT THIS GROUP
OF CUSTOMERS

They buy what you sell, but not (yet) from you.

They're currently with the competition.

Life is not nearly as good with the competition as it would be with you.

They know your name, and you know theirs.

They will remember you when you call them.

This is a warm call, not a cold call.

It's a friendly call.

It's a feel-good call.

Let's go help them!

WHY CALL THEM?

We call prospects we've talked to previously because it is the implementation of our perseverance.

It is what we do, but our competition does not.

It creates a desire within the prospect to reward us with business.

People appreciate multiple efforts because they mean you care enough to try repeatedly.

For the prospect, of course, it would be a benefit to work with you instead of the competition. They'd be better off for it.

For you, this work feeds your pipeline.

It opens opportunities and progresses them.

It brings in fresh customers with new needs that you can help with.

It's a joy.

How lucky are we to get to do this work?

Your Script: What to Say to Prospects You've Previously Talked To

The Opening

Hi Samantha, it's Manny with XYZ Co. It has been a while since we talked – how have you been? How's your family? Kids doing okay? How's business going?

The Shift to Business

I was thinking about you because I have a customer similar to you, and they were placing an order the other day for some of the services (or products) you and I had discussed. How are you doing with those services (or products)? I'd love to help with them.

Now, an rDYK:

What are you buying from other suppliers that I can help you with?

or a DYK:

Did you know we do service x and service y? Would love to earn your business on that.

And another rDYK:

What kind of projects do you work on that I can help with?

and another:

What do you have coming up? Would love to help.

You don't have to ask all of these questions, just the ones that feel right to you. Or ask your own.

Now, Pivot to the Sale

Well, I can put together an initial quote by end of day and get it over to you. When can you get me the P.O.?

Or, schedule the next conversation:

When would you like to talk about this again?

or try to schedule a meeting:

I'll be in your area next week, Wednesday and Thursday – which one is better for you? Would love to connect and continue this conversation.

Ask and listen.
Get your answer.
These prospects need you.
Don't hurt them by not letting them benefit from your value.

When we do not communicate, that is what we do to our customers and prospects – we hurt them.

When we call people proactively when nothing is wrong, we appear before them almost like a miracle, presenting them with a better way, a dependable partner, and incredible value.

PICK UP THE PHONE SUCCESS STORY

"Every Sunday, I sit down and go to my call notebook, and I make a list of people I will try to call this week. It's a time when I think through what's coming up and who needs to hear from me. I follow your script, and whether I actually talk to them or just leave a message, I always tell them I was thinking about them. Almost all of them call me back and tell me how nice it was to hear from me. The key to making these calls for me has been to have the people listed in my call notebook. That's my place to plan my calls. I do it on Sundays, and then I reference it throughout the week. My sales are up nearly 200% this year, and there's no doubt that planning these calls, and then doing them, has been a big reason for this."

—Martha Z.; inside sales, distributor

PART FIVE

COLD CALLS: CALLING PEOPLE YOU DON'T KNOW . . . YET

CHAPTER

33

An
Important
Note
on Cold
Calling

This part of the book explores cold calling, which is the commonly accepted term for calling people you don't know. But I don't want you to think of these calls as cold calls.

This next four chapters will lay out why *there are no cold calls.*

You have a lot in common with your prospects, even the ones you don't know.

So don't think of them as cold calls; think of them as human calls.

Think of them as relationship calls.

Think of them as *helping calls* that will help *you* and your sales effort, but that mostly will help your prospects tremendously because they will be presented with the opportunity to benefit from your great value.

For this, they are lucky.

CHAPTER 34

THE
BENEFITS
OF CALLING
PEOPLE
YOU DON'T
KNOW . . .
YET

P roactive calls to current and past customers are the lowest-hanging fruit in revenue growth.

The next most effective group to call are prospects who know you or your company – or at least would recognize you or your company – but have not yet bought from you.

And finally, we have the least effective – but still important – group of people to call: prospects who do not yet know you. These prospects are covered in the next few chapters.

What important role do calls to prospects you do not yet know have for us salespeople?

Calls to people you don't know create more people you do know.

These calls fill the pipeline, expand your opportunities, and build your bench of prospective customers.

When you make these calls, you also get to help more people, which is no small thing.

Let's explore the benefits – for us and for them – of calling prospects who do not yet know you.

PROSPECTS DON'T KNOW YOU ONLY ONCE: AT THE BEGINNING OF THE FIRST CALL

Salespeople have huge and understandable discomfort about calling people we don't know – but these prospects don't know us only once. As soon as they pick up the phone and you introduce yourself and tell them who you are and what you do, they know you.

Then you can use some of the warm-up techniques described in the coming chapters, and they'll know you better.

By the time you end your first call, you'll have gotten to know each other. You will no longer be strangers.

And when you call the second time, they will know you.

They will remember you.

Because nobody has called them like you have. Before you call, you will have done your research. You will know something about the person and his or her company. And you will have some stories and examples prepared about *your* customers and how you've helped them.

This will be memorable and singular for the prospect.

They don't know you only when they pick up the phone for the first time and say hello.

CALLING PEOPLE YOU DON'T KNOW QUICKLY BUILDS THE LIST OF PEOPLE YOU KNOW

Calling prospects you haven't talked to previously quickly expands the number of people you know.

And if you call these folks strategically – calling customers of your competition, for example – you *know* they need what you sell even before you talk to them.

So, you're building your list of qualified prospects who need your products, services, attention, timelines, accuracy, and dependability.

YOU'RE FILLING YOUR PIPELINE AND INCREASING YOUR OPPORTUNITIES

When you call people you don't know, you're filling the left (early) side of your pipeline.

Customers can go away: they retire; they move on; they shift part of what they do to someone else.

Folks you don't know today become your future customers and can be replacements for your current customers.

More prospects in the pipeline mean more opportunities.

More opportunities mean more people to call, build relationships with, and follow up with.

Opportunities are the lifeblood of a salesperson's success.

A full pipeline will almost always feed your family well.

MORE PEOPLE WILL GET TO BE HELPED BY YOU

You get to deliver more of your value to people who need it.

This is no small thing, so don't underestimate it.

Right now, these prospects are *not* being served at a level you and your company provide.

By calling on them, you are providing them with an opportunity for less worry, decreased errors, time savings, decreased expenses, and increased profit, and you allow them to serve *their* customers better.

This is what you do in the world.

Now it's time to let more people benefit from it.

CHAPTER

35

There Are No Cold Calls, so Stop Thinking About Them That Way

P eople often ask me about how to make cold calls, and in my reply, I almost always include that I don't believe there are any cold calls.

I think we have a lot in common with the people we are calling.

This was true in normal times, before the pandemic, and it is especially true post-pandemic.

In fact, I think we have so much to talk about with prospects we don't know that we can talk for *an hour* about things we have in common before even getting to business.

So, let's review all the things we have in common with our "cold call" prospects.

Please keep these things in mind when it's time to call somebody you don't know.

You know a lot more about them than you think.

You can ask about all of these different areas in a casual getting-to-know-you conversation.

PERSONAL AREAS IN COMMON

In these areas, you can share first if you'd like and then ask the prospect about themselves. Or vice versa – whichever feels more comfortable.

Family: You're both working to take care of your family and provide for them as well as you can. *How is your family doing?*

Kids: Ask about somebody's kids, and you will honor them, and they might talk to you for 10 minutes or more about their children. *Do you have kids? What are they doing?*

Home: You both have homes to take care of, no matter what kind of place you reside in. Here, you can volunteer something: *We have been remodeling our master bath, and it seems to be going on forever.*

Vacation: They take vacation and time off, just like you. You can ask them what they did.

Travel: They've been places, and when people go places, they love to talk about it.

Hobbies: Everybody has interests outside of work. *I'm a big vegetable gardener, so that's how I blow off steam in the summer months. A new pursuit for me there: I grew a giant pumpkin for the first time last year – it reached 420 pounds, which was quite small by giant-pumpkin-growing standards. I will try again this year.* (All of this is exactly true.)

PANDEMIC AREAS IN COMMON

The pandemic itself: This is a powerful and intense shared experience that we all went through together. On my calls with people I don't know, this is a topic that comes up frequently. *How did you and your family do during the pandemic?*

Health: Is everybody healthy? If somebody in their family had Covid, how was it? What about co-workers – have they successfully avoided Covid?

Kids in school: *Did the kids make it back into school? How did they do with remote learning?*

Business during the pandemic: *How did the company do during the pandemic? How was it selling without being able to see your customers?*

Working from home or office? How is that? *Did you enjoy working from home? Are you still? Are you looking forward to getting back into the office?*

Have things gone back to how they were? Will they? *Are things back to how they were at your office? Will some people keep working from home?*

BUSINESS
AREAS IN COMMON

Customers who are angry: Just as you have customers who bring your problems and urgencies and, at times, anger, they do too. You can connect over this. *I wanted to pick up the phone and call you when nothing was wrong! I bet you don't get a lot of those!*

Salespeople who only call when they need something: Salespeople call customers rarely, and usually when something is wrong. *I didn't want to be the guy who called only when he needs something. Yes, I provide products or services that you buy (I've done that research), but first, I wanted to connect so we can get to know each other and make sure I can add value to what you're doing.*

You Have All This in Common – So Please Stop Thinking About Them as Cold Calls

Look at all of the areas I just listed.

You and I don't know each other, but we can talk about these things for an hour – without even getting to business topics – or even longer over a beer.

Thinking of it as a "cold call" instills fear, costs you money, and hurts your company.

A cold call is a negative effort right?

"I have to make cold calls now" is a sure way to *avoid* making the important calls that will fill your pipeline and demonstrate your value to more people.

So let's not think of these as cold calls any more.

Let's think of them as relationship calls.

Let's think of them as helping calls, because that's what you do.

Think of them as connecting-over-all-we-have-in-common calls.

Think of them as opportunity calls.

Think of them as calls you are grateful to make.

We're lucky to make these calls, and the recipients are lucky we have selected them to try to help.

They may not know they're lucky yet, but they will soon. And that's a fun part of the work – to help them realize they're lucky!

You're making relationship calls.

You're making helping calls.

CHAPTER 36

How to Find Prospects You Don't Know Yet

Now that we've covered why there are no cold calls, especially in our post-pandemic world, let's look at how to identify new prospects to call. This chapter covers where to find and uncover new prospects.

Ask Your Current Customers *Who Else* Buys What You Sell

Most salespeople assume that their customer is the only one in the company who buys what they sell.

In many cases, there are other people who also buy it.

These alternate, additional buyers can be in other offices or different regions, or they might be sitting right next to your buyer.

Sometimes your buyer goes to you, but her colleague goes to *his own* supplier. The only way to find out is to ask, and you may be pleasantly surprised.

Here is your language:

"Who else at your company can I help the way that I help you?"

or . . .

"Who else at your firm buys what you buy? I'd love to help them, too."

This is called an *internal referral:* you are asking to be connected to somebody else inside the company who would also benefit from buying from you.

ASK YOUR CURRENT CUSTOMERS FOR REFERRALS OUTSIDE THEIR COMPANY

This is a request for a connection to a buyer at another firm. Many times, salespeople don't ask for referrals because we are afraid to ask the customer to connect us with their competition. If you are seeking to avoid this, simply disarm it on the front end:

"Who do you know, like yourself but at another company that doesn't compete with you, who I could help the way that I help you?"

As with all direct questions, ask and be silent. Wait for an answer. Don't speak until it comes.

One critical thing to remember with referrals is that your happy customers would *like to* give you referrals. They are pleased with your work. They have friends or colleagues elsewhere who would benefit from your work. If they connect you, their contact is helped by you, and you are helped by the business. In turn, you will go out of your way to help the referring customer. Everybody wins, but who wins most of all? Who looks best in that exchange? The referring customers!

People love to give referrals.
Help them do what they love by asking!
Don't take that away from them.

ASK KEY CONNECTORS FOR REFERRALS

Who can refer you to your ideal prospects?
Lawyers and accountants?
Architects?
Engineers?
Go to them.
You know a number of these folks already.

To connect with more of them, consider offering a lunch-and-learn session for their office. (Bring lunch, if you're feeling benevolent.) At this event, you can talk about how your firm works with their clients – your target prospects. Explain how their clients would be improved if they worked with you and how great you would make the referrers look. Not only will you feed them, but you will also make them look incredibly smart for connecting their clients to you!

MINE YOUR COMPANY'S PAST CUSTOMERS

These do not have to be *your* customers, merely those who once purchased from your company. They are the perfect prospects to call and introduce yourself to, and let them know you'd like to help them.

> "Hi Tom, it's George Moulder with ABC Company. How are you? I know we haven't talked before, but I noticed that you used to buy from us on a regular basis. I wanted to let you know I've been here for four years, and I would be honored to help you personally and take care of your account. Are you still using products x and y?"

Present it as a fresh start for your firm's past customer, and let them know you would like to oversee their account personally.

They will be impressed, because it's quite possible nobody has ever told them this.

Ever.

CALL PROSPECTS YOU SIMPLY KNOW ARE BUYING ELSEWHERE NOW

There may be prospects in your area who you simply know are buying from the competition.

You probably know about the significant potential customers in your neighborhood (or target market) who are doing business with competing suppliers or service providers.

They're not buying from your company, but you know they're out there, spending money – and struggling accordingly – with the competition.

Find their number, and call them.

Introduce yourself.

Tell them you've done your research, and you know they buy what you sell, but they're obviously not buying it from you, and you would like to change that.

> "What would it take to earn your business? I would love to help you our way. We've had a number of customers come over from this company, and they've all commented about how we are more available, by cell phone, at all times. And I'll return your call in the evenings, and on weekends, too."

IF YOU NEED EVEN MORE, GO TO LINKEDIN

If you need to find even more prospective customers to call, go to LinkedIn.

Many of the people who buy your products and services are there.

Some of them even list their phone number in the contact information they provide on their profile.

You can send them a LinkedIn message, which, as discussed earlier in this book, works significantly better than an email. In your message, be sure to detail other customers like them who you help, and what they buy, and make sure the products or services you list are similar to what you think this prospect might need.

They're on LinkedIn to find value for themselves.

You can provide immense value to them.

Offer it there.

The worst that can happen is there's no reply, or they say no – in which case you've lost nothing, and you've tried to help.

And welcome to the cold prospecting game.

We have to walk through a lot of no's to get to a yes.

So, take another step and keep walking, head held high, with confident belief in the tremendous value you bring to your customers.

PICK UP THE PHONE SUCCESS STORY

"I love asking my customers who else they work with who I can help. That's how I like to ask it – *who do you work with?* It's one of my favorite questions because the customer will almost think of another employee at his company, or a customer, or a supplier, who I can help. I sell services, so I can help all of those people. It's a great question because it lets the customer pick people to connect with me. My customers know what I can do. It's to their benefit to send me their friends so I can do the same for them."

—Chris P.; third-party administrator, financial services

CHAPTER 37

SCRIPTS FOR QUICKLY WARMING UP COLD CALLS

Here is your language for calling prospects you do not know.

These calls are in four parts, as opposed to the calls to customers and prospects who you do know (those are laid out in the previous part of the book and have three parts).

The four parts of this conversation are as follows:

The opening: Introduce yourself, and build familiarity.
Warming up the cold call: Address the areas you have in common, listed in Chapter 35.
The shift to business: Move the conversation to products or services you can help with.
The pivot to the next commitment or the sale: Secure the date of the next interaction or the business.

YOUR SCRIPT: WHAT TO SAY TO PROSPECTS YOU DON'T KNOW (REMEMBER, THESE AREN'T COLD CALLS, BUT RELATIONSHIP CALLS OR HELPING CALLS)

The Opening

Hi Tom, it's Alex Goldfayn with the Revenue Growth Consultancy. How are you? Listen, we haven't talked before, but my good customer brought up your name and asked me to reach out to you, so I wanted to pick up the phone and connect with you.

or . . .

Hi Tom, it's Alex Goldfayn with the Revenue Growth Consultancy. How are you? I'm calling because I currently work with your colleague George Smith in Department X, and he thought I should reach out to you too and see if I can help you the way that he and I work together. So I wanted to pick up the phone and call you.

or . . .

Hi Tom, it's Alex Goldfayn with the Revenue Growth Consultancy. How are you? I'm sorry we haven't connected previously, but we're a wholesale distributor here in town and are known for the personal attention we give our customers.

We work with companies like x and y in the area, and they always talk about how the orders are timely and how they appreciate that we are available whenever they need something, even in the evenings and on weekends. You're a big contractor in town, so I wanted to pick up the phone and introduce myself. I'd love to help you the way that I help companies x and y.

Warming Up the Cold Call

After your prospect answers some of these questions, share your experiences as well. Don't just fire questions, but make it a conversation.

Your responses and reactions to their answers are in italics.

How has the pandemic gone for you guys?

We've done surprisingly well here. Our customers didn't need us any less during that time, certainly. But how we interacted with them certainly changed, like it did for everyone.

Has business done okay during this terrible time?

That's great to hear, Tom. I'm glad you've done well. That could have been an incredibly difficult time for business, so it's tremendous that you've come through it so well.

Has your family come through it okay, Tom?

Same here. We had some family come down with the virus around the country, but luckily nothing within our house.

How did your kids handle school?

What a challenge for everyone. The whole generation will be affected by this, but at least they all went through it together. Luckily, everyone experienced similar things at the same time.

The Shift to Business

Start with some rDYK questions:

So what products do you buy from the other guys, Tom? I'd love the opportunity to help you.

or . . .

What kinds of services do you use from contractors like us? I'm interested to see if we can help you. I know we'd sure like to.

Now go to some DYKs about products and services that they are likely to need.

We provide products like x, y, and z. Do you have ever buy those kinds of things?

or . . .

We also have a lot of customers who take advantage of our services a and b. Would that be useful for you?

The Pivot to the Next Commitment or the Sale

I've really enjoyed our conversation, Tom. What's a good time for me to stop by with samples for you to take a look? Would love to meet you in person as well.

or . . .

> *It's been great talking with you, Tom. Let me get some pricing over to you, and why don't we schedule our next call while we're talking? How's your Monday at 2 PM to reconnect briefly?*

or . . .

> *Thanks for the great conversation, Tom. I'll write all this up and get a quote over to you in the next 24 hours. When do you think I might expect the P.O.?*

Again, you don't have to use my language.

In fact, the sooner this becomes your language instead of mine, the better you will do.

Take these prospects through the conversation in a relaxed and easy-going manner.

Be comfortable, not nervous.

The worst that can happen is that you will be in the exact same place you were when you picked up the phone – and that's a pretty good place to be.

They're lucky to be talking with you and have a shot to benefit from your value.

Go into the conversation with that confidence, and just try to help these folks the best you can.

That's the work.

And it's pretty great work, isn't it?

PICK UP THE PHONE SUCCESS STORY

"It's amazing how we're all going through this [post] pandemic time, and I can talk to pretty much anyone about it. I get on the phone with people I've never talked to before, and we can talk for 15 minutes about how we're dealing with Covid. Inevitably, the conversations move to the products they need, and before you know it, lo and behold, they put in their order. What's the lesson? Keep connecting with people. People *need* that connection. If you're not calling, you're probably not connecting. People *want* to talk. Then they buy."

—Sarah Y.; customer service, mechanical contractor

CHAPTER

38

LET'S FOCUS ON WHAT WE CAN CONTROL

As salespeople, we cannot control if the customer will buy.

Whether they say yes or no is not within our control.

We can try to influence their answer.

We can do everything right, ask all the right questions, and present our value in a compelling – and the customer may still say no.

In sales, nearly everything is outside of our control.

We can't control if the customer will pick up the phone or not.

We can't control if our customer is having a good day or a bad day when we call.

Did they have an argument with their spouse or significant other?

Did their boss treat them unfairly today, right before our call?

What about budgets? Have they been cut?

Sometimes the customer simply disappears for weeks and months, only to return, oddly, as if nothing happened.

Lots of people can tell us no all the time, but very few people can tell us yes, and only sometimes.

And all of this is nearly entirely outside of our control.

We can't control much in the sales profession, but we can control our effort.

We can control how frequently our customers hear from us when nothing is wrong.

We can control expressing that we are interested, that we are present, and that we care.

And because our family relies on our success in this work over which we have almost no control . . .

And because our company relies on us to generate sales in this job in which we have so little control . . .

We should do everything we can to implement the behaviors we *can* control.

Behavior follows mindset – what we do is totally determined by what we think. So we should get our mind right.

We should be clear that the worst that can happen is not so bad.

We should understand the incredible value we bring to our customers and prospects.

We should move from fear to confidence, and from avoidance to enthusiasm and gratitude.

We can decide to think this way and work on making sure we think this way.

We should be bold, and then we should behave accordingly.

We can control picking up the phone and offering to help our customers more.

We can control telling our customers we'd like to help them and asking them what else they have coming up that we can help with.

Because if we do this, the rest will take care of itself.

We will maximize our chances for success.

Our opportunities will grow exponentially.

Our pipeline will fill.

You can't get hits unless you swing the bat.

Each proactive call is a swing – at helping your customers more.

More swings always – *always* – turn into more hits.

Your proactive calls tell your customers that you care.

Your proactive calls tell them you want to help.

We owe our customers this effort.

We owe this effort to our company.
We owe this effort to our family.
We owe this effort to ourselves.
We are in total control of this effort.
What a blessing!
Control what you can control.
And everything else will take care of itself.

ACKNOWLEDGMENTS

My friend and editor Richard Narramore at John Wiley & Sons is exceptional at his work, but perhaps he should have been an entrepreneur. He has excellent ideas all the time, and I get to benefit from them constantly as this is our fourth consecutive book together. The last two became *Wall Street Journal* bestsellers, so something is working. I suggest it's mostly Richard.

Wiley is an excellent partner for me because they work fast, and I do too. The idea for this book was put together in late December 2020, I turned in the manuscript in mid-March 2021, and it hit the market exactly six months later in September. Other publishers don't work this way. I want to thank Wiley vice president and publisher Shannon Vargo for adding her creativity and brainpower to this work. I was lucky to have it, and the book benefited a great deal.

Thanks, as always, to the rest of the great team at Wiley for all they do and contribute: Victoria Anllo guarantees timelines, or else (in a good way); Deborah Schindlar moved the book through the publication process deftly; Michael Freidberg provided excellent marketing support; and the excellent copy editor, Tiffany Taylor, who has handled my last two books, turned my manuscript into the clean, correct book you're reading now.

Anyone who knows my story knows that it's built on the backs of my parents, Leon and Jane Goldfayn, who dragged our small family out of the communist Soviet Union in 1978 while in their early 20s, with basically no money, or English language, or connections. I was two years old when we came to the U.S., and because my family spoke Russian at home, I had a heavy accent until I was about 10 years old. In a lot of ways, I was able to build my business – also without any connections, right out of college, in those early and difficult days – because I watched how my parents built their lives: with hope, optimism, and endless perseverance. My dad recently retired, but my mom still goes to work daily. I try hard to honor them in my work today.

My 95-year-old grandmother Bella taught me to see the bright side in everything because that's what she still does, every single day. It's amazing to witness, and we're all lucky that we get to learn from her, even now.

I lucked into a tremendous family-in-law in Ron and Jan Lobodzinski, and my bro-in-law Keith. We like to garden and drink wine and eat well together. I am grateful for their support, always.

My wife Lisa and I are lucky to have friends who have become family to us: Jeanne, Greg, and Sean Livelsberger, our original neighbors three houses ago, have been close to us for over 18 years. The time we got to spend with Kendall and Ben Haight, along with Myles and Ainsley, over this past year helped tremendously to get us through this most difficult pandemic time. And we are very lucky to have the hugely generous and amazingly caring Saqeena Haq, Amir Contractor, and Ifti in our lives. We are grateful to these families for their love and support and can only hope we return it sufficiently.

I am fortunate to benefit from the friendship and support of fellow entrepreneurs like Wes Trochlil, with whom I can banter all day about business and politics; Chris Patterson, who has provided invaluable counsel – and belief in me! – for almost 20 years now; and Jeff Conroy, who sees things clearly and correctly every time I asked him for advice. Thank you, gentlemen.

Many solo consultants find themselves isolated and lonely, but I never feel that way because I have exceptional clients I consider my friends. I am grateful for the partnership of Paul Kennedy, Mike Meiresonne, Greg Guy, Karl Hallstrom, KayCee Hallstrom, Paul Van Duyne, Jeff Kenton, Bryan Huston, Brent Bernardi, Frank Rotello, Don Maloney, A.J. Maloney, Christy Maloney, Patrick Maloney, Michael Maloney, Gary Bernstein, Ted Lerman, Carl Parker, Jeff New, Jordan New, Dan New, Ben Hannewyk, Charlton Keultjes, James Roth, Renee Roth, Nick Brister, Doug O'Rourke, Michael Whiteside, Mike Adelizzi, Mike Miazga, Matt Sanderson, Chris Mundschenk, Lee Self, Matt Glaser, Kevin Gammonley, Rick Johnson, Dennis Madden, Bill McDonough, Tony Hutti, Aquiles Nunez, John Ackroyd, Jon Cruthers, Glenn Perkins, Ric Franzi, and Ron Penland. Thank you for your trust and support.

My executive admin, Dana Luparello, has adjusted to her role quickly and well, and she keeps the small things running efficiently so I can concentrate on my clients and proactive calls. Thank you for your dependability, Dana, and for increasing mine!

I also want to thank Marisa Cali and Dan Disney for their support and dedication to my mission. I am thankful to have you both on my team!

The next three people are my *why*. They are my reason for taking risks in business and persevering. My daughter Bella and my son Noah may teach me more than I teach them. They're only 12, but sometimes they produce insights and connections that adults would be lucky to make. You kiddos are my joy and my inspiration.

And my bride of 20 years, Lisa, has heard countless of my business ideas over the years. They only see the light of day if they get past her, and almost none do! She is my sounding board and my best friend, my muse, and my consigliere. And she's an exceptionally talented cook, to boot! How lucky am I? Thank you isn't enough.

ABOUT THE AUTHOR

Alex Goldfayn grows companies.

He is the CEO of The Revenue Growth Consultancy, which works with organizations to install positive mindsets and systems of simple behaviors that routinely generate an additional 10–20% in new sales annually.

His clients include manufacturers, distributors, and business-to-business service organizations, typically in mature industries – which make the world go around. Revenue growth projects with Alex run typically run for 6 to 12 months and include multiple in-person and remote learning experiences for your customer-facing teams, as well as detailed tracking, scorekeeping, accountability, and recognition components.

Alex's projects aren't sales training, but sales doing. He builds mindset and behavior habits for your customer-facing teams.

Not only does Alex regularly implement the systems in this book for his clients, but he also applies the approaches in his own firm, one of the highest-grossing and most successful solo consulting practices of any kind in America.

Throughout the year, Alex delivers more than 75 workshops and keynote speeches for companies, executive groups, and associations.

In addition to *Pick Up the Phone and Sell,* he is the author of

- *5-Minute Selling* (2020) – WSJ bestseller
- *Selling Boldly* (2018) – WSJ bestseller
- *The Revenue Growth Habit* (2015) – 800-CEO-Read Sales Book of the Year
- *Evangelist Marketing* (2011)

Alex lives with his wife and 12-year-old twins in the Chicago area.

If you'd like to discuss your firm's growth with Alex, please call him directly at 847-459-6322 or email alex@goldfayn.com.

INDEX